## Florence Bramford R.V.M. (Royal Victorian Medal) 1891–1985

Against a backdrop of British history, this book presents the life of Florence Bramford, who became a Ladies' Maid to the Ladies in Waiting of *two* Queen Elizabeths, from 1939 to 1974.

This is the life of my great aunt Flo, as related mainly by herself through my aunt, Margaret Bramford. Great Aunt Flo had a Victorian childhood and an Edwardian adolescence. She was privileged to reside in many a royal residence with her Ladies in Waiting and was frequently invited to serve on Royal Tours all over the world. Her efficiency, enthusiasm, and good humour were much appreciated by all who knew her.

*Richard Lyntton (Né Richard Bramford)*
*Philadelphia, 2022*

# *From*
# COTTAGE
# *to*
# PALACE

Margaret Bramford

A Malchik Media & richardlynttonbooks Publication

*Published by*

**Malchik Media & richardlynttonbooks**

Copyright © 2022 Richard C.G. Lyntton

ISBN: 978-1-7354905-2-6

Cover and interior repackaging by Gary A. Rosenberg •
www.thebookcouple.com

*About the cover image:*

The Royal tour signed group photograph on the front cover features Florence Bramford (circled) with King George VI, Queen Elizabeth I, Princess Elizabeth (Queen Elizabeth II), and Princess Margaret on *H.M.S. Vanguard* en route to South Africa in 1947.

Thank you in advance for reading
*From Cottage to Palace ~ Book 1*

• • • • • • • • • • • • • • • • • • • • • • • • • • • •

For more information about the **Worcestershire & Malvern History Series** by Margaret Bramford, or to sign up for our FREE richardlynttonbooks Reader Regiment newsletter, visit the richardlynttonbooks website:

**https://richardlynttonbooks.com/contact/**

# Contents

• • • • • • • • • •

# 1 ~ A Victorian Childhood

"George! George! Come quickly! Bang the dustbin lid! The bees are swarming!", shouted seven-year-old Florence, wearing a long white pinafore and sturdy buttoned boots.

It was noon on a Saturday in May 1898. Florence was running down the straight path of the long Worcestershire garden and banging together a saucepan and its lid. This was called "tanging" the bees.

Her brother George, nine years old, dark-haired, attired in his everyday knickerbocker suit and boots, soon followed her, making a commendable din. He looked like a mediaeval knight of Newbridge Green, striking his shield, the dustbin lid, with a stout stick.

The children's noisy duty on this fine May morning, in a hamlet close to Upton upon Severn, was to make their father's swarming bees settle in his garden, rather than in the field or orchard. A more experienced bee-keeper down the lane would then come to put the swarm back in the hive.

Florence and her brother were brought up on honey. Their father had three hives. Their mother sold honey. Before the end of May, a lady called Miss Anderson from The Glebe, would make her regular visit to their cottage and ask, "Have you any virgin honey?" By this, she meant early, pale honey.

"Good! They've settled on our apple tree," exclaimed George. "Dad will be pleased," remarked Florence, quietly.

1

Their duty done, the girl and her brother looked fleetingly towards the blue Malvern hills in the distance. This was their favourite view.

Then they ran back to the house, past the long orderly rows of well-tended vegetables, the pink blossom of the apple trees and along the brick paths, lined by low, well-trimmed box hedges, which exuded a spicy aroma after summer rain.

Florence went back to the cottage kitchen to scrub the new potatoes for dinner. George ran down the lane to tell the bee-keeper about their swarm, before returning to the stay behind the cottage, where he was "cleaning out the pig".

Florence, named after her maternal grandmother, was the eldest daughter of George Bramford, who originated from the village of Laxton in Nottinghamshire, a truly mediaeval village. There, even today, they still operate the Open Field system, whereby the farmers cultivate strips of ground in different parts of the village.

Son of a Laxton farmer, and born in 1862, George Bramford had been recommended by the Reverend Henry Martin of Laxton, as "a promising young man", to be coachman to Colonel Sir Charles Johnson of The Hill, Upton upon Severn, in Worcestershire.

Lady Johnson, one of the Martin family of Ham Court, close to Upton, was a relative of this Laxton Rector. Servants, in those days, were often hired purely on the recommendation of relatives and friends.

"The Reverend Henry Martin had high standards," so George Bramford used to relate. "If he saw a flyspeck on his carriage window as he set off to visit a lady, he would ask his coachman to return home to have the window cleaned first. He was a good Vicar at Laxton. He was there for forty years.

The poorer villagers would be given soup and blankets from the Rectory."

Thus, young George Bramford from Laxton came south to Upton upon Severn and remained in the service of the Johnson family for the rest of his working life. With his upright, spare figure, clean-cut features, alert and steady gaze, George became a capable and reliable coachman.

He looked smart in his navy blue livery, with white breeches for special occasions. The coachmen of each big house in the district could be identified by their distinctive livery the colours of their uniform. For Ham Court, it was green with red collars. The livery of Madresfield Court was red and black, while at Pull Court, Bushley, it was fawn.

Florence reminisced:

"Dad would drive the spring cart into Upton almost daily for groceries for The Hill. In the afternoons, he would drive his master and mistress to call on friends the Cherrys at Henwick, the Isaacs, or to catch a train at Upton station.

"On some days he might be driving a passenger or a parcel to one of the big houses nearby -The Hyde or The Boynes. Otherwise, he would be grooming the horses, cleaning the stables, the coach and the harness a never-ending job."

Florence would see her father sometimes, riding one horse and leading another, as he exercised them down Southend Lane, opposite his cottage, or took them to the blacksmith at Longden Heath. He would return home at the end of the day, smelling of horses and polished leather and still wearing his leather gaiters and strong boots.

"Best of all, George and I were allowed to ride in a cart with Dad, on special occasions. I remember how we would meet a train at Christmas and collect parcels of food for the Home of the Good Shepherd at Welland. My father's Lady Johnson was Patron of this Home. We children, wrapped in travelling rugs, would accompany Dad in the open cart, along the Hanley Road and back through Welland."

Soon after young George Bramford had arrived at The Hill, there had appeared a young lady, neat and lively, with dark hair and twinkling dark brown eyes. Eva Alice Wills had come to be lady's maid to Lady Johnson's sisters who also lived at The Hill—Miss Ranira and Miss Jemima Martin, whose family home was Ham Court.

The young coachman from Nottinghamshire began noticing Eva as she went about her duties, for she would have to warn him when to be ready with her ladies' carriage. Her sparkle and decisive manner were an attraction to the calm, responsible young man with the serious face.

Eva's father, John Wills, also had twinkling dark brown eyes above his beard. He had been Station Master at Bradnich, Devon, where Eva was born in 1864, and then Station Master at Crediton. He was next appointed as Chief Clerk at the Harbour of the flourishing port of Bridgewater, Somerset.

Eva Alice often talked about her father's Bridgewater office, and his tall desk with a hefty ledger on it. "Looking outside, I would see the harbour alive with sailing ships, each with their brightly painted figureheads." The Harbour Master's house can still be seen near Bridgewater harbour.

The courtship at The Hill went well. George and Eva had their engagement photos taken by Norman May of Malvern. Eva Alice wears a velvet bustled dress, a brooch and a locket, looking roguish and a trifle vain. George wears a cutaway coat and waistcoat with covered buttons and a gold horseshoe tie pin. He gazes equably on the world.

They were married in St. Mary's Church, Bridgewater, on the 4th of June 1888. Their wedding photo, in the studio of H. Davey of Exeter, shows George in new pinstriped trousers, waistcoat hiding a fob watch, jacket with bound edges, winged collar and spotted silk tie. He is seated on a cushioned chair, upholstered in plush, with long cord fringes, beside a potted palm. From his direct gaze and firm mouth there flowed confidence and trust.

His wife stands at his elbow, her hands resting on his forearm, showing her engagement and wedding rings. She wears a dark dress, beaded with jet and has an ample ruched bustle. Her hair is swept up; she wears tiny earrings and a brooch. From her "Spanish" face, with full lips, her prominent eyes look soulful and a little apprehensive.

They were to set up home in a brick cottage with oak beams on the Ham Court estate. Their cottage had once been a "one up, one down", with stairs leading directly from the front door. In the 1870's the cottage had housed a Dame school, kept by old Mrs. Cowley for the local children. As a young man, George Bramford had been her lodger.

# 2 ~ Home in the Cottage

The Bramford's ancient cottage is still very much in existence. Brick-faced in the eighteenth century, it has a half-timbered inner structure, which may well be Elizabethan or Jacobean. The oak beams, hand-cut, still retain small pieces of bark. The elm floor of the oldest bedroom is likely to have been used originally as timbers of a ship.

The plaster on the interior walls was recently found to contain horsehair, proclaiming its age.

The cottage is marked on a map dated 1701, looking like "a little shed". The Drum and Monkey Inn, next door, is not marked on that map, showing it is less old.

"The annual rent," said Florence, "which my father paid in 1890 was £6.14s and there was a pigsty in the back yard. Everyone kept a pig in those days and lived off the salted sides of bacon for months. I well remember the bacon and the chine (the backbone) being hung on hooks in the kitchen."

And now, one hundred years later, the cottage proudly bears the name BRAMFORD COTTAGE because the Bramford family had lived there for 93 years continuously.

In 1888, with the prospect of a family in view, the landlord decided to extend the cottage at the back, to include a kitchen and an extra bedroom. So the newly-weds moved temporarily to a dark house in nearby Monsell Lane, until their cottage extension was completed.

A description of their home in the Catalogue of Farms on the Ham Court estate, in 1914, reads as follows:

"A Capital Detached Cottage Rent £6.14s p.a.
(the rent had remained unchanged since 1890!)

Kitchen—tiled floor, range and cupboard

Parlour—tiled floor, fireplace

Back Kitchen—tiled floor, closed range and copper

Pantry—tiled floor

Three bedrooms, two with fireplaces

Piggery with court

Timber and tiled coal shed

Brick and tiled earth closet.

Let to Mr. G. Bramford on a tenancy terminable at any quarter-day by three months' notice."

Florence remembered the baker's oven in the front kitchen, where they used to bake bread.

I myself well remember seeing in the original pantry, a cool, dark room, the large earthenware pots in which my grandmother kept the bread.

My father, George Henry, first-born of the Bramfords, arrived on May 17th, 1889, and grew up accustomed to drawing water from the outside pump, which never ran dry; collecting eggs from the hens in the orchard; scratching the back of the pig; running to the outside closet with wooden seat in its brick "house" and being bathed in front of the kitchen fire.

He was to have a playmate on April 8th, 1891, when his sister, Florence came into the world. Both children had the long oval face of their father and the dark brown beady eyes of their mother. Miss Ranira Martin, godmother of baby George, would come from The Hill to the cottage to see the babies of her former ladies' maid being bathed in the back kitchen.

As a baby, one winter's day, Florence was wheeled in her wooden pram by her mother, right on to the River Severn at Upton, and across to the other side. The river was frozen over! Her father and others skated seven miles down the Severn to Tewkesbury, in the great frost of 1891.

Florence recalled her childhood. "We used to play all sorts of games in the garden. We used to like to be bakers because the bakery next door used to fascinate us with its bread and oven. I had a little box with a little string on it. George was the baker and he made mud into little loaves and put them under the plum tree to bake. I used to take the loaves round to the other plum trees who were our customers!"

"We used to have hoops. I had a large wooden hoop and George had an iron one with a hook on the side to guide it, you see. On Saturday afternoons we used to say to Mother, 'Well, can we go to Longdon?' She used to say, 'Well, you be careful!' So I would bowl my big hoop across the road and George on the other side would bowl his smaller hoop so that it came through my hoop. We used to go all the way down the Langdon Straight like this. So it shows there wasn't much traffic!"

When Florence was three years old, a new baby, Mabel, arrived. A family photo shows all three children in front of the cottage, where white roses climb up to the bedroom windows.

On November 4th, 1897, when Florence was six, a grand wedding took place in Upton upon Severn. Miss Eleanor Mary Bromley Martin of Ham Court married Mr. Robert Martin Holland-Martin of Overbury Court, Worcestershire, in the parish church of Upton.

Little girls aged five or six, living on the Ham Court estate, were selected (or perhaps requested!) to be flower girls at the wedding. Florence was one of these.

She remembers it vividly. "We were all dressed in white. There were about six of us. We had white baskets and white flowers and we had to strew the flowers in the aisle when the bride came down after the wedding. Outside the porch, there was an awning down to the gate."

"From the porch, under the awning, stood a file of older girls, up to twelve or fourteen years of age. They were dressed in red cloaks with green hoods. That was the livery colour of Ham Court. They had chrysanthemums of that shade red, brown and bronze, which they strewed where the bride walked, under the awning, down to the gate. It was in November and it was a lovely day." A very Victorian wedding indeed!

Six sons were subsequently born to Mr. and Mrs. Robert Holland-Martin: Geoffrey, Edward (known as "Ruby"), Cyril, Derek, Thurstan and Christopher.

Florence was destined to make frequent stays at Overbury Court, their family home, in the course of her duties, later on in her life.

# 3 ~ Florence's Schooldays at Upton upon Severn

· · · · · · · · · · · · · · · · · · · · · ·

On May 14th 1895, at the age of four, Florence Bramford went to school for the first time, in charge of her brother, George, aged six. They had a mile and a half to walk, along a quiet road.

Florence recalls her school days. "The Girls' school was over the Infants' school. Our Girls' school Headmistress was a Miss Dobson. She was there for many years and was a very nice person. We were separate from the boys. But I always remember we could hear the boys reciting 'The Old Year lies a-dying.' They used to say their poetry aloud sometimes. We would hear them when we were out in the playground. We learned poetry by heart then and we used to sing quite a lot of songs."

"We took sandwiches with us every day for lunch and also an apple and a bottle of milk. Sometimes it was dripping sandwiches if Mother had nice beef dripping. Otherwise, it was a bit of bacon, but always an apple because we had plenty of those. We used to sit in the schoolroom by the fire and have our meal, then go out and play afterwards."

"When the floods were out, we would be watching the water every day. If the water came over the road, at the bottom of Tunnel Hill, we couldn't go to school! I always remember a big wagon came from Guildings, Southend farm, to take us home from school at half-past three in the afternoon, because the flood water was coming over the road. Nobody could walk through it. It was very exciting for us all!"

George was a diligent and attentive pupil. He was later to become a Pupil Teacher in that same Upton school. "He was a very good teacher, liked by all", says one of his Upton pupils, Austin Hartwright. "He was very gentle, never ruffled, and always had a smile. He had his father's looks and even temperament. I can see him now, as plain as punch!"

George was eventually to train at Saltley Training College in Birmingham, to teach at Cromwell Street school in the Nechells district of that city, and to become Headmaster of two Worcestershire schools, first in Overbury and then in Pershore.

Florence, meanwhile, was also a conscientious pupil. She was improving her needlework skills on samplers, at school and at home. "Mother said I must be occupied."

The sampler she embroidered in cross stitch at the age of nine or ten, includes two small crowns in red and the likeness of a Royal Yacht in blue all symbols of her future. In later life, Florence was to have strong links with crowned heads and the Royal Yacht Britannia.

She also knitted lace. All this anticipated her apprenticeship to a milliner and her skill in repairing dresses for her Ladies.

Florence's Head Teacher in the Infants' school, was Miss Priestnall, who had 154 infants on her books. To assist her, there was one other qualified teacher and two Pupil Teachers Julia Pockett and Rose Edwards, aged 15 or 16. They were paid the noble sum of £7 per year.

Her Majesty's Inspector's report at about this time, comments, "The Infants' Department is conducted with great vigour and considerable success."

"The children's hats, caps, etc. must on no account be allowed to hang in the schoolrooms. Extra cloakroom accommodation (including a lavatory) should be at once provided. The infants now use the same offices as the girls in the separate Girls' school, although there is no special accommodation therein for the wants of infants." (no chamber pots!)

Life was hard in those days, for four-year-old Florence and her classmates. To gain access to some smelly earth closets, used by about 300 pupils, you had to line up also with girls aged 8–14.

"The offices (i.e. earth closets) are extremely malodorous," said Her Majesty's Inspector on October 24th 1895. "They are a source of danger to the health of children and teachers alike."

It was not always gloomy, however. Lady Johnson, wife of Sir Charles Johnson, a school governor, occasionally visited the school and distributed toys among the infants.

Little Florence would be very impressed by a visit from this gracious Lady, seeing that Florence's father was Lady Johnson's coachman. He would have driven Her Ladyship in her carriage from The Hill to the school.

The infants' teachers did their best for their charges. One entry in the Log Book reads, "Prepared coloured straw and paper for 'babies' to thread, as an occupation." There were Kindergarten games too "The Little Housewife" and "The Pigeon House", and Musical Drill, with scarves or dumbbells. Flag drill too was taught.

Florence would be learning new songs such as, "Tommy's Army" and "Dolly Dear". A harmonium was brought from the Boys' School for singing lessons so that they could practice "See us dance our stately measure."

There were other dances too. In January 1898, "Commenced teaching a polka." In October 1899, "I chose the Swedish Dance."

Victorian songs taught to Florence and her class were "Merry Little Maids and Merry Little Boys", "The Seasons", and "The Swing". For a recitation, they learned "The Fly's Bath". The little boys did Drawing while the little girls did Hemming.

An important and weekly feature of the timetable in those days was the Object Lesson which we would now regard as Environmental Studies. Upton's Infant School Log Book of 1893-1912 discloses an interesting list of Object Lessons that were to be taught every year:

| | |
|---|---|
| An Umbrella | The Clock Bees |
| A Postage Stamp | A Railway Station |
| The Cow | Feathers |
| The Camel | India Rubber |
| The Elephant | The Mouse |
| The Ostrich | A Candle |
| The Robin | Thimbles |
| Bread Sugar Milk | Beasts of Burden |
| The Baker | The House-fly |
| The Grocer | Pins and Needles |
| The Farmer | An Iron Kettle |
| The Shoemaker | About ourselves |
| The Blacksmith | Moon and Stars |
| Money | |

The "Candle", "Iron Kettle" and "Blacksmith" jolt us right back into the Victorian era.

The weather greatly affected both attendance and classroom conditions:

*May 25th 1895* Weather very wet. A good fire was lighted in the classroom.

*September 10th 1895* Weather very hot. No drill given.

*October 28th 1895* The schoolroom is very cold. The boy who attends to the fires has been very neglectful." (By February 4th 1896 a caretaker had been engaged.)

"*November 14th 1895* A terrific storm of hail and rain. Children thoroughly wet. I sent home children in accordance with Official Letter Code G 94/27675 Article 12. Register not marked."

Illnesses were frequent in Florence's childhood, and parents dreaded the doctor's bill. The Infants' Headmistress had to record Whooping Cough, Measles, Mumps, Diphtheria, Chicken Pox and Ringworm, at various times.

On October 15th 1894, Mrs. Priestnall wrote nervously that there was an epidemic of Scarlet Fever, one of the most feared of illnesses then. "The classroom has been well disinfected with carbolic acid and a wet sheet hung there."

Maintenance of buildings seemed to be arbitrary. The school governors of this Church of England school had to juggle with the budget. The disappointment of Florence's Headmistress is manifest when she writes, after the Harvest Holiday, in August 1895:

*"Re-opened, after four weeks holiday. School floor has been scrubbed. and walls swept. In the Boys' and Girls' departments, walls have been painted and coloured. The School Correspondent*

*has said that the Maintenance Dept. had not ordered decoration for the Infants' school, as it was last done in 1888." (That was seven years ago!)*

The school was lit by gas from brackets. School furniture was not always reliable. On March 25th, 1897, "New desks from Birmingham Educational Depot are not nearly as strong as our old ones. All the screws are getting loose."

The treatment of the school piano is revealing:

*"April 30th 1895* Piano lent for Mothers' Meeting entertainment in Town Hall and it has not been returned."

*"May 1st 1895* Piano brought back this morning in a heavy shower of rain, with no covering. Owing to it being continually lent for entertainment, it is being very much damaged. The back is very much broken and will have to be repaired."

Poor Headmistress! She had much to suffer, including the reasons for her pupils' absences, which ranged from "Hop picking," "Blackberry Picking," "Pea picking," to "Minding babies" and "Travelling on a coal barge with my mother." The river Severn, in those days, had a much more industrial use.

Some pupils were troublesome in other ways:

*October 18th 1895* Punished a boy this morning for stealing sweets from a basket in the porch. This boy was punished two days ago for taking pencils from the school cupboard."

*"May 19th 1896* Kate … is continually coming to school in a very dirty condition. I have had to send her home several times to be washed. Several parents have asked that their children be kept from sitting by her. I have reported this case to the Rector, the Relieving Officer and the Nuisance Inspector."

Miniature holidays enlivened the school routine. On Ash

Wednesday, Florence and her school-mates would be shepherded to church, as was the custom for church schools. They even had a holiday for Michaelmas Day, September 29th (a Quarter Day).

Local events in Upton upon Severn often dictated reasons for holidays. A half-holiday was accorded for the November 1897 wedding of "Miss Martin of Ham Court". Florence, of course, had her own invitation to this wedding, as one of the little flower girls, which she has already described in chapter two.

*April 17th 1896* Upton Races in afternoon. Only a few children presented themselves. Did not open school." The same kind of entry was made on the day of Tewkesbury Fair and when a Circus visited Upton.

National events also left their mark on schools. Thus, when Florence was six years old:

*June 18th 1897* Queen's Diamond Jubilee. School closed till 28th Jun. (Ten days!) Tea, sports, fireworks." When Florence was nine:

*"May 21st 1900* Holiday all day to celebrate the relief of Mafeking. Children assembled and sang God Save the Queen and were then dismissed."

The Worcester Diocesan Inspector's termly report on the important subject of Religious Knowledge:

"Children bright, intelligent and well behaved. An excellent tone throughout the school. The silent fag end of the class should be decreased, however."

The role of the Rector in church schools was quite a significant one. The Rector at Upton upon Severn took regular Scripture lessons. But he had other functions as well: "The Rector called and heard recitations and watched Musical Drill." "The

Rector took the school Shoe Club money on Monday." "The Rector sent a large basket of sweets."

Other local worthies visited the school also: "Mrs. Lawson gave the Drawing prizes."

"Mrs. Martin of Ham Court called and kindly promised to send plants for the school."

It was a sad day when "the pupils stood in the playground to sing a hymn, during the passing by of the funeral of their late teacher, Miss W. Gibbs."

But in class, Florence and her fellow scholars were singing lustily such songs as:

| | | |
|---|---|---|
| The sleigh bells | | The Scarecrow |
| The Minstrel Boy | and | I'd choose to be a daisy |
| Tit Willow | | If I were a sunbeam |

On Empire Day, May 24th the girls sang patriotic songs and saluted the flag in the playground.

Florence's mother, Eva Bramford, was determined that Florence should win one or more of the prizes for Needlework, donated annually by George Bramford's employer, Lady Johnson. There was much supervision and encouragement of Florence's sewing at home, by her mother. There were several categories for Sewing prizes: Back-stitching, Buttonholes, Gathering, etc.

On December 19th 1900, aged nine, Florence was thrilled to receive a prize for Back-stitching, from Lady Johnson. On June 30th 1904, aged thirteen, Florence was given First Prize for "Marking" in Sewing.

Good attendance was also rewarded by Lady Johnson. At the age of eleven, in 1902, Florence received a book for "Never missing school for one year." Her sister Mabel's First Prize for Buttonholes at age thirteen is also recorded, as is her book prize for unbroken attendance for one year. Their younger sister, Winifred, aged ten, was listed in 1910 as "among the best in her class in Religious Instruction."

But the Bramford girls all had to look up to older brother George, Pupil Teacher in the Boys' school. His excellent results in the Diocesan Pupil Teacher examinations are frequently mentioned in the school Log Book. It was in 1908, at the age of nineteen that he left for Saltley Training College, Birmingham, to qualify as a fully-fledged teacher.

He returned to teach in his old school at Upton, from 1910 to 1913, and was, on two occasions, in his early twenties, placed in charge of the Boys' school, when the Headmaster was ill as George himself records in the Log Book.

On November 3$^{rd}$, 1913, it is recorded: "Mr. G. Bramford has left the school. He will be much missed, having taken a great interest in his work and also in the boys."

## Sunday School

Florence recalled going to Sunday School at Ham Court. "We had to go every Sunday. The two Miss Bromley Martins were our teachers and also Miss Anderson who lived at The Glebe, nearby. There were three classes, in different rooms. We always went to the Smoke Room. Another class was held in the School Room. We always had to learn the Collect of the day. Each one had to go and recite the Collect after a hymn. Then we had a reading out of the Bible and another hymn."

"Then we would go into the Scullery where there was always a very large cake baked in a tin. It was a sultana cake cut into big portions. We were all given a piece of cake and a cup of milk."

"One day, the children threw their cake to the chickens. There were a lot of chickens there. So the next Sunday, Mrs. Martin was there, of all people! The old lady, the mother, gave a lecture to us all. She said that if we didn't want the cake, we were not to give it to the chickens. We were not to take it at all. She was very upset. The cake wasn't baked for chickens, anyway!"

# 4 ~ We Entertained Ourselves

"When I was a child," said Florence, "Russians would come round—generally two men, with a bear, chained to one man. Outside our cottage there was a little three-cornered piece of grass, where "the corner boys" stood while they were waiting for the pub to open."

"The Russians would sing a Russian drawl of a song and the old bear would get up on its hind legs and dance with its owner. The other Russian had a stick and he would give the bear a little whip up now and again to make it keep on dancing."

"At other times there was a man with a monkey and a funny little organ which he carried on his back. When he put it down on the ground, it stood on one stick in the middle. The organ was carried on one shoulder and the monkey on his other shoulder. The man turned the handle of the organ to make music."

"You had to go up to the monkey and give it a penny. The monkey would take a little paper out of the side of the organ and that was to be your fortune, you see! The monkey was dressed up in a skirt and a sort of cape with a funny little hat on its head."

"Then there was the German band a brass band. It used to play on the corner as well. So that was our entertainment when we were children!"

The Bramford family, like many others of that time, were

adept at providing their own music. Father George had a good tenor voice and he played the violin and melodeon. Before they acquired a piano, he would accompany the children's songs and dances on his violin. His son George, taught himself to play the piano and later learned to play the organ. He was a good tenor singer too. Florence would sing contralto and play duets with her brother. She had piano lessons until she was fourteen. Florence's party piece was to sing Down the Vale.

Mabel's was to sing Feed the Birdie. George's solos were Men of Harlech and The Lost Chord.

The whole family would gather round the piano on their return from Evensong in Upton church, to sing hymns. Father George was a true Christian and what was termed "a good Churchman", which meant "a regular member of the church choir". He sang in Upton parish church choir for 50 years. A silver tankard was presented to him to commemorate this achievement just a few months before he died in 1934.

On one of the old choir pews of Upton parish church a plaque reads:

*In Memory of*
GEORGE BRAMFORD
1861–1934
*who for nearly 50 years was a faithful chorister
and worker in this church and parish.*
R.I.P.

Florence's father also sang in Upton Choral Society, which was conducted by Miss Madeleine Bromley Martin of Ham Court. "She was very musical," said Florence. "It was Sir Edward Elgar who taught her to play the piano. He would come by train from Malvern to Upton, and a carriage would meet him at Upton station to take him to Ham Court to give his piano lessons."

"Miss Madeleine's Choral Society held their rehearsals and concerts in the Town Hall, now called the Memorial Hall. They used to practice one night a week. Dad always used to laugh about one incident. They were singing the Psalm, 'As pants the hart for cooling streams.' Miss Madeleine stopped them. She said, 'Now tenors, you are not getting off your pants quick enough!' There was a great joke about that!"

"I worked at Ham Court and I joined the Choral Society because Miss Madeleine recruited Lydd Webb and myself to sing. When we were at Sam Hill, Bushley, with the Martin family, we used to have morning prayers every day at nine o'clock, before they had their breakfast. Mrs. Martin read the prayers and we sang a hymn."

"Miss Madeleine suddenly discovered one day that Lydd and I had got voices so we had to sing the alto. We had to stay behind every morning and have a little practice. I liked singing alto very much."

There were plays too in the Town Hall, Upton. Florence's brother, George, took the part of Robin Hood in a school concert there. He was appropriately cast, as his father hailed from Nottinghamshire.

Christmas was a very special time for homemade entertainment. Florence had vivid memories of Christmas as a child.

"We always used to go to The Hill for Christmas Day. That was our invitation from Sir Charles and Lady Johnson for the whole family to go up there for Christmas dinner. We would go at about half- past twelve dressed up in our best. I had to learn a piece of poetry to say to Lady Johnson after our lunch. We had a very nice turkey lunch and then we had to go and receive our Christmas present."

"I had to say my poetry to Dad first to make sure it was all right and proper. I think George, your father, had to do something else as well he probably had to sing. Then there was always a lovely Christmas cake for tea. All the house staff were together in the big hall and we would stay there till about seven o'clock at night."

"We had our own Christmas parties in the cottage too. The blacksmith lived about half a mile away and also the Head Gardener of Ham Court and their families. The Head Gardener had two children and the blacksmith had three, and they used to come here to the cottage.

"We would have a wonderful big tea. Then it was all cleared away and we all played games. We had a lot of singing to the piano in the corner over there. We did a bit of dancing too. It was great fun to dance with the grownups!"

"Then George and I always had to play a duet. I remember once we did The Minstrel Boy and another time we did a lovely waltz. I was playing the top part and George was playing the bass. We sang carols too."

"The next day, we went down to the Watkins', the blacksmith's house for a party. Then we went on another day to the gardener's house."

"Mrs. Carr, the gardener's wife, was most amusing and a very funny person. She always used to dress up. One time she came down with Mr. Carr's pajamas on and a straw hat and banjo and she sang us a little song."

"Another time, she came dressed up as a gamekeeper with a gun under her arm anything she used to borrow things from different people! We thought it great fun because she would disappear and we would say, 'Oh, she's gone to dress up!' And she'd come in, you see, and perform."

# 5 ~ Growing Up, With Uncles and Aunts

• • • • • • • • • • • • • • • • • • • • • • • •

When Florence was nine years old, she was sent to her father's sister, Aunt Nance Taylor, in the village of Laxton, Nottinghamshire, for some months in the summer. Florence went to the village school there and played with her friend Claire Merrill among the castle ruins.

She recalls: "One day, I went with Aunt Nance, Mrs. Merrill and Claire in a pony-drawn trap to Newark market to sell eggs and butter. Aunt Nance drove with Mrs. Merrill at her side. I sat with Claire behind, facing backwards."

"Aunt Nance and Uncle William were "pillars" of the local Chapel. They often gave hospitality to visiting Methodist preachers. I had to read from a large, illustrated Bible at the family service in the house each evening when we also sang hymns."

Florence also sang in the Chapel Choir at Laxton, where Uncle William was himself preacher and curator. But everyone seemed to attend both Chapel and church in those days! Village boys were compelled to sing in the church choir in the morning and in the Chapel choir for evensong. Bill Bramford, farmworker and brother of Aunt Nance, was organ blower in the church for most of his life. He was paid every quarter for organ blowing.

25

In Laxton parish church, there is an oak vestry door to the memory of the faithful Chapel leaders, Aunt Nance and her husband, William Taylor.

People in Laxton still remember Aunt Nance (Aunt "Tet" as she was known). She was born in 1846 and was a much respected, religious woman, who helped others. She wore her long old-fashioned skirts, petticoats with big pockets, and her sun-bonnet, right up to 1937, when she died.

Aunt Nance had a little shop in her house, where she sold butterscotch and homemade sweets, giving to children generous portions for one penny. For Sunday school picnics, her caraway seed cakes and marrow jam tarts were famous.

I still cherish the 1880's clothes worn by Aunt Nance, which include her best black silk cape adorned with jet beads and her best black bonnet trimmed with gold wire. Laxton village retains, even today, its medieval atmosphere. On a warm May evening, there is a delightful scent from flowering currant hedges lining the village street and swallows twitter as they swoop over the many farmyards.

I was shown an ancient branding iron with the initials HB on it. This was what Henry Bramford, Florence's grandfather had used to brand his sheep. A Laxton farmer told me: "We bought sacks named 'Bramford' at their farm sale and they lasted for years."

When she was fourteen, Florence left school and was apprenticed to a dressmaker and milliner in Upton upon Severn. she had to cross the old stone bridge over the Severn to reach the house of Mrs. Hartwright, who had several pupil apprentices.

Florence's father always met her in the town at half-past six in the evening, to escort her home to Newbridge Green, because there were no lamps at all! "Once you left Upton bridge, you were in darkness. So Dad walked home with me."

Mrs. Hartwright had three children at that time. The youngest, Austin, needed attention, while his mother laid out the work for her young apprentices. So Florence was chosen to nurse the little boy, meanwhile. Austin became, in due course, a pupil of Florence's brother and later worked with Florence's father on Saturdays.

"I had a young aunt, Rose Wills, in Bridgewater," recalls Florence. "Rose was the youngest sister of my mother. Once, when I visited the Wills family in Bridgewater, Rose made me thread needles for her and pick up pins from the floor."

The Wills of Bridgewater, Somerset, provided Florence with seven uncles and aunts. There were Aunts Harriet, Flo, Laura, Louise, Rose, and Uncles Jack and George. In those days, when diphtheria, meningitis and T.B. were killer diseases, few families were spared, however numerous their offspring.

So it is not surprising to learn that three of the Wills, Harriet, Jack and Rose, died of T.B. in early middle age. Jack was to leave behind a Sunday School prize a beautifully illustrated copy of John Bunyan's Pilgrim's Progress, which I treasure.

Florence said: "Uncle George Wills, who was only ten years older than me, would come each summer to stay in the cottage with us at Upton. He would enliven the place with his witty sayings. He was always quoting from Gilbert and Sullivan operas and he would often play the piano and sing Edwardian Music Hall songs."

"He would always hide a penny when he left to go home and we children would have to find it. Once it was poked between two pieces of wood on the yard fence. Another time it was weeks before we found the penny tucked under the stair carpet!"

This Uncle, in later life, was a keen astronomer and had his own telescope in his garden. He would acclaim the wonders of Venus, Jupiter, and Mars and revel in the Milky Way.

He was also an avid reader of classic novels. The lifelike characters of Hampshire and Dorset, created by Trollope and Hardy, were familiar friends to him, coming as he did from that same area of South West England. He would announce, with a twinkle in his dark brown eyes and a green book in his hand, "I'm taking Mrs. Henry Wood to bed with me!"

Florence now had two sisters. Mabel had been born in 1894 and Winifred Rose in 1901. Mabel was to become a children's nanny, but alas! typhoid fever claimed her at the age of 27. Winifred also became nanny to two little girls. She survived T.B. and reached her eightieth year, living most of her life in the cottage at Newbridge Green.

# 6 ~ Some Upton Upon Severn Characters

• • • • • • • • • • • • • • • • • • •

The Bramford children would sometimes walk from New-bridge Green to Upton along the old road. They went down Southend Lane and along the old Roman causeway which leads from Southend Farm and Ham Court.

There had been a Roman settlement near Portmans Farm, where several Roman coins had once been ploughed up in a field. The Bramford's friend, Ruth Jakeman, the farmer's wife, had once found an opaque, very pale blue stone brooch in an antique setting after a field had been ploughed.

Florence and George knew well that the "old road to Upton" was said to be haunted by bold bad Captain Bound, riding on his grey horse. He was a Puritan landowner of seventeenth-century Upton, cruel and covetous of land. Detested in his lifetime, because by night he removed other people's landmarks to benefit himself, he was feared even more after his death, for his haunting of the old causeway where he used to ride.

Florence relates: "Old Granny Tudge, well known to local residents, would frequent the old Roman causeway, imbibing her bottle of gin. No ghost was she but she did love spirits! She would rest in a spinney on Portmans Farm, taking all Saturday to walk from an Upton pub to her home in Stanks Lane, Longdon Heath."

"As she reeled past the gate of our cottage, she would see Dad over the hedge, working in his garden. Waving her bottle, she would call out cheerily to him, "I like it, I do!" wait on the little green in the early 1930s for the pub to open. It was then kept by John Fawke, who pleased himself about opening times.

As a child, I myself remember seeing him. He was then a very elderly man, living alone, amid the cobwebs and dust of the dirty, unkempt and eerie tavern, lit by oil lamps. My aunt Winifred would bring him meals. He gave my little sister, Avril, a silver coin.

Old John had the bushy grey beard of Victorian times and his yellow, incredibly wrinkled old face, peering out of the shadows, resembled that of a monkey. "He only needs a drum!" the customers would comment, in their Worcestershire accents. It was also rumoured that old John's wings were hanging up in the barn!

After John Fawke's death, in about 1932, Florence's father "kept the license open" for a few months, and acted as barman until a new innkeeper was appointed. They were still using oil lamps.

The newly painted inn sign of The Rose and Crown*, in pink and gold, soon sprouted a little brown drum and a little grey monkey in the bottom corners. In a few years' time, a new inn sign was commissioned and this time the Drum and Monkey predominated.

The change of name had been dictated by a persistent piece of local folklore! Later, the old bakery became a skittle alley. Later still, the barn became a restaurant.

"As children", said Florence, "our greatest treat in summer was to be taken for the afternoon on the train from Upton to Malvern, to walk on the hills. We would arrive outside the

Imperial Hotel at Great Malvern and would walk up Avenue Road to the Winter Gardens, where a band was always playing. Then up we climbed to St. Ann's Well, to ride on some docile donkeys up to the Beacon."

Old Betty Cleveley lived at Barley Cottage in nearby Queenhill. She had been born in 1796. At Upper Lode, near Bushley, Betty Cleveley's s job was to carry sacks of barley off the boats. The Severn was very much used, in those days, for ferrying cereals.

Florence's father used to relate: "On Betty Cleveley's one-hundredth birthday, many callers from neighbouring farms came to see her in her cottage, to wish her well and bring her presents."

"Betty was discussing her son, then aged 73, who was ill. She remarked, "He was always delicate. I thought I would never rear him!" "Well, he's had a good innings!" was her listeners' reply. Betty retained all her faculties and her memory and she lived to be 103. She is buried in Queenhill churchyard.

Another anecdote concerned Ham Court, sold and dismantled in 1914. There was a painting in one room, depicting Cleopatra and the Asp. When asked which painting he liked best, a local man used to say, "Cleopeter and the Wops."

Miss Ranira Martin of The Hill, to whom Florence's mother had been Lady's Maid, was known to be rather eccentric. "As there were no handbags in those days, this lady would wear a belt, from which dangled her jingling keys, her umbrella and her purse. This was considered to be an unusual fashion!"

"When Miss Ranira went away to stay with friends, she would always take with her a top hat covered in cretonne, to use as a waste paper basket. She would use a doll's dustpan on her bed-head, to deflect the light, so that she could read in bed."

"Sometimes, at weekends, George and I were allowed to accompany 'Grandad Smith', a gardener at The Heath, on the train to Malvern Wells for a little holiday. We would all stay the night with Mr. Smith's son, who was in charge of the Golf House on the common. There would be a bar there for golfers in the evenings. George and I would sometimes act as caddy on the golf links, or play ball games on the common."

"George and I would sometimes act as caddy on the golf links, or play ball games on the common."

---

*Footnote: By tradition, local farmers used to meet in the Rose and Crown to agree the price of their hay. Today, as a reminder, small bales of hay hang from the ceiling in the Drum and Monkey.

# 7 ~ Stately Homes and Haunted Houses

•  •  •  •  •  •  •  •  •  •  •  •  •  •  •  •  •  •  •  •  •  •

In the early 1900s, "going into service" implied joining a whole echelon of staff, in a country house on an estate, or a townhouse of some size and status.

While performing your duties as children's nanny, governess or lady's companion, you were expected to be on good terms with the housekeeper, cook, maids, butler, valets, coachman, grooms and gardeners, all of whom you would meet in the course of your work. A camaraderie and friendship developed, between employer and servant and between servants themselves, akin to that of a crew on board ship.

Florence's first post, at the age of fifteen, was at Ham Court, as Under Ladies' Maid to the two Miss Bromley Martins, her former Sunday School teachers. She was given £12 a year and paid quarterly. Of course, she thought she was rich!

Ham Court was a delightful eighteenth-century mansion that had been designed by Anthony Keck. It was described as "A Gentleman's Residence", which had 90 acres of well-timbered park, 150 acres of water meadows by the River Severn, and 10 Capital Farms. The Bromley Martins had had Ham Court built. It was completed in 1772.

The same Anthony Keck designed the cupola ("the old pepper pot") of Upton upon Severn's old church. He was a leading architect in the counties of Worcester, Gloucester and Hereford. Highgrove, near Tetbury, home of the present Prince of Wales, is another of Keck's designs. Ham Court's interior was described as having elegantly carved mahogany doors, marble mantelpieces and a solid oak staircase. Outside, there was a tennis lawn and a sunken garden.

It is strange and sad to reflect that this stately home was sold on October 27th-28th, 1914, dismantled and shipped to the U.S.A. Only the stable block remains.

Having a father employed as a coachman and a mother as former ladies' maid, and living on the Ham Court estate, it was natural that Florence should be recommended, at the age of 18, as lady's companion and dresser, to a lady related to the Martins of Ham Court.

Florence relates: "They thought it was time for me to move away somewhere else. So I was sent to Mrs. Evelyn Martin, the sister-in-law of Mr. Martin. She was a widow with a daughter and living in London. I went in 1911 to London first. I was with her until she died."

"We lived in London until the 1914 war. The daughter got married in 1915. She married a sailor and he was stationed outside Edinburgh. Mrs. Martin was very devoted to her daughter, Mrs. Stewart, her only child. So we moved up to Edinburgh in a little house near the daughter and lived up there all through the war."

Mrs. Evelyn Martin, as she was known, came from the Ledbury branch of Martins. Her father, Chairman of Martins Bank, would travel by train to London each Monday and back each Friday. The Ledbury Martins who lived at Upper Hall, until recently the home of Ledbury's High School, had nine children in the family.

The work of a "dresser" does not imply dress-making. It includes pressing and preparing clothes, with their appropriate accessories, ready to wear. It involves making repairs and alterations to dresses; liaising with the laundress or dry cleaner; caring for jewelry.

A dresser must pack her lady's clothes, carefully folded in tissue paper if she is going away. On arrival at her destination, the dresser unpacks and presses the clothes all over again.

Being a dresser and lady's companion is often tedious, and only a person with a high degree of integrity, loyalty, discretion, resourcefulness and attention to detail would be efficient and happy in such work.

Florence Bramford was admirably suited to her task and responsibilities. Mrs. Evelyn Martin (whose Christian name was Edith) was very satisfied with her young companion and dresser. She treated her almost as a daughter, and Florence cared for her mistress and remained with her for 25 years.

It was a sociable life and a status symbol to be serving the gentry in those days. When she was not accompanying her lady to London or to large country houses to stay with friends, Florence was talking to and working with the rest of the staff. They all took pride in their jobs. Thus she was acquiring a fund of wisdom, experience and good humour in the world of gentlefolk and their retainers.

There were great advantages "in service" if you had a kind and reasonable employer good accommodation, ample meals, companionship, travelling to unusual places, home-spun entertainment ... It was an education to broaden one's horizons. So many servants were employed in the big houses of that period, that life was never dull. "It was great fun!" commented Florence.

"We were amused to hear one of our hostesses rousing her maids at five in the morning. 'Get up my maids! Get up, my maids! Praise the Lord! Praise the Lord!' But the lady of the house would then go comfortably back to bed, while her maids did all the work!"

One of Mrs. Evelyn Martin's residences was The Heath, Longdon. Another residence was at Sam Hill, Bushley, near Tewkesbury. While waiting for alterations to be carried out there, the household moved for three months to stay at Homme House, Much Marcle, in Herefordshire.

On their Sunday off-duty, once a month in summer, the four Upton-based staff, including Cranton, the coachman, would cycle home together the seventeen miles from Much Marcle to Upton upon Severn, to spend the day with their parents and families. Then on Sunday evening, the quartet of cyclists would meet up and peddle the seventeen miles back to Much Marcie.

With her lady, Mrs. Martin, Florence stayed, at various times, in several stately homes of Worcestershire, including Pull Court. She stayed four times at Madresfield Court. It was the era of visiting friends for weekends, among the gentry; a constant exchange of hospitality among "people of quality". Mrs. Martin and Florence were always "on the move"!

Homme House, Much Marcle, was thought, by at least one housemaid, to be haunted. This maid would not enter one of the rooms after dark, as she felt she was being watched. So she closed the door of this room well before nightfall.

Upper Hall, Ledbury was also said to be haunted by the ghost of a former owner. Florence would have to wait up until 11.30 p.m. sometimes, to help Mrs. Martin take off her dress, and then return to her own bedroom. The following morning, the housekeeper would always ask Florence, "Did you see Old Skyppe last night?!" The answer was always "No!"

The Skyppe family had lived in Upper Hall from 1542. In 1812, Penelope Skyppe had married John Martin of Overbury Court hence the Martin family's connection with Upper Hall. It is, however, a certain Lady Katherine who has been seen several times in the past, on the stairs outside the Black Prince's room in Upper Hall. Her history is unknown. (see footnote 1)

One night, Florence told me, one of the ladies of the house was frightened by "a dreadful sight" in the corridor of Upper Hall and she fainted. The Hall is on a monastic site, close to the parish church. It is thought by some that there is a passage from the cellars of the house to the church.

What is certain is that the present house contains a mediaeval house inside it, because the foundations of the house date back to 1200, declares a local historian.

"Doors would mysteriously open, on still days, in our classroom in the old stables," I was told recently, by a former teacher of the John Masefield High School, based at Upper Hall.

"There are presences there," declared Florence. "During the First World War, Upper Hall was a hospital. Mr. Martin turned part of the house into a convalescent home for wounded soldiers. There was a sister there, a V.A.D. nurse. One nurse came from London. Her father was a General, I think."

"She only stayed there two days. She said, 'I can't stay in this house any longer. It's so haunted: Everywhere I see all these people. I sit down in the dining room and they're all round me.' So she must have been very psychic, mustn't she?" (see footnote 2)

"I stayed over at St. Briavel's Castle once, down near

Chepstow. That was haunted, they used to say. They would ask if I'd seen a ghost. And I would say, 'I'm afraid I haven't!'"

"Dick Guilding, when he was a small boy, living in Southend Farm, Newbridge Green, said to his mother, 'Who's that man who comes at the bottom of my bed?' But nobody knows who he was or anything about him. It's a very old house, Southend Farm."

"At Ham Court, there is the grey lady. My sister Win and a friend saw it going towards the river. That ghost is in Puritan dress. Then there is the house in Upton called Soley's Orchard. That's haunted by Captain Bound."

Another "ghostly" episode took place at Hillend, on the way to Castlemorton, where Winifred Bramford was looking after an empty cottage for friends. She had cycled there to light a fire, ready for their return.

As she opened the front door, she heard a dreadful scream from upstairs. After a minute, she steeled herself to climb the stairs, gingerly, and peeped into each of the bedrooms. In one of them, perched on a wardrobe, was an owl! She released it through the window.

---

Footnote 1: This Lady Katherine is not thought to be the same as Saint Katherine, patron saint of Ledbury. She was Lady Katherine Audley, a cousin of Edward II. She came to Ledbury, found the bells ringing without ringers, and consequently built a hermitage near The Hazel. There she lived a saintly life to the end of her days. A fourteenth-century tomb in Ledbury church is reputed to be hers.

Footnote 2: In Victorian times, there were lively accounts of skating on the Upper Hall pool sometimes by the light of fires.

# 8 ~ The Horseless Carriage Arrives

The age of the motor car had dawned! In Upton upon Severn, Doctor Nash, the local doctor, was the first to drive a car to visit his patients. His car had an open top and a canvas hood.

It was now time for coachmen to be transformed into chauffeurs almost overnight. In about 1912, Florence's father, George Bramford, like many other coachmen, was sent to the Austin works in Birmingham, to stay for a week or two. He had to learn not only how to drive, but also to maintain Colonel Johnson's newly acquired motor car.

Then, a Birmingham man came to stay at The Hill, in Upton, for a month, to instruct and accompany the newly fledged chauffeur, Mr. Bramford, as he drove his master in the new vehicle, at 30-40 m.p.h. through the Worcestershire lanes.

In a few years, Colonel Sir Charles Johnson died. His widow moved to a smaller house, opposite The Eades in Monsell Lane. The Eades was the family home of the Tennant family, of whom Admiral Sir William Tennant, Lord Lieutenant of Worcestershire, was the most famous.

Lady Johnson decided to banish all her carriages and horses in favour of a very smart car a Daimler. Austin Hartwright remembers it well.

Austin was the Upton boy who had been minded, as a baby, by Florence Bramford and taught by her brother, George.

Austin left school at the age of thirteen, came to work for Lady Johnson, alongside her chauffeur and earned about ten shillings a week in 1913 which was very good pay in those days.

Austin recalled to me that period in his long life: "I worked in Lady Johnson's house and cleaned the silver and the pewter candlesticks. I had to scrape the old candle wax out of each candlestick and wash them all in hot water, ready for lighting candles at night."

"I helped the parlour maids and cleaned the shoes. I was expected to collect letters from the Post Office from Lady Johnson's private box."

"She was a smart lady, Lady Johnson, a nice old soul, very active. It was 'Yes, my Lady; no, my Lady', of course. Then I would help the gardener, Ernest Bennett, to sift soil and pot geraniums. Another job was to feed the geese."

"I well remember the Daimler, because I had to help your grandad, the chauffeur, to clean it, but I never had a ride in it. It was a beautiful car, with real leather upholstery, standing in what had once been the coach-house. Your grandad was always cleaning and polishing it ready for the drive out. It always looked like new. He looked after it like a doll! Mr. Bramford would stand by the car in his smart navy blue uniform, down the long drive from the front door. The parlour-maid would wave, and that was the signal for him to drive up to the front door and help her Ladyship into the car. He would drive her to Upton, Hanley, Ryall or Malvern. She was always going out for a drive."

Young Austin would visit the Bramford's cottage and be offered a cup of tea, on his way to the blacksmith's.

"She was sweet a real nice person," Austin says of Florence's mother. "I got on well with her." Of Florence's father he says,

40

"There was nothing blustering about him. He had a rare old laugh. Your grandparents were real nice folk."

Florence, too, learned to drive a car in the 1920s in Ireland! It was Mrs. Edith Martin's Rover, with a hood which rolled back. During her six weeks holiday back in England, in 1928, with Mrs. Martin, she was taken to Cheltenham to hire a car from Haynes and Strange, so that she could get further driving experience.

Florence remembered with what pride she drove her parents that summer from their Newbridge Green cottage, through Tewkesbury, to Overbury, at the foot of Bredon Hill. They were visiting her brother, George, his wife and little daughter, aged four, in the School House at Overbury.

As a small child, I can dimly remember this auspicious occasion. I had scarcely seen a motor car close up before. The cars owned by the Holland Martins of Overbury Court went slowly and smoothly past our house. But this one was actually parked in our school playground!

Of course, no driving test was needed in those pre-war days. You just bought a licence for five shillings and a friend or relative gave you driving lessons!

In Ireland, in the mid-1920's, Mrs. Stewart, who had been teaching Florence to drive her mother's Rover car, thought it was time for Florence to experience Dublin traffic.

They came to a crossroads and a Dublin policeman holding up the traffic. Florence forgot where her brake was, in her excitement. She crawled forwards, very slowly, edging the policeman out of the way, over the crossroads!

Being Irish, he did not mind and he just laughed. He let Florence off with a warning. If you could drive in Dublin traffic, you could drive anywhere!

# 9 ~ Florence in Ireland

●●●●●●●●●●●●●●●●●●●●●●●●

After the first world war, Florence accompanied Mrs. Edith Martin to Killiney, Co. Dublin, to live in a house called Otago. This house was a few minutes' walk from the home of Mrs. Martin's daughter and son-in-law, the Stewarts, and their three children, Rynn, Colin (a girl), and Sheila. Florence and Mrs. Martin lived there until Mrs. Martin died in 1935.

Florence was marvelous at amusing the children when she was not too busy. "We used to visit Granny about once a week," recalls Sheila, "and usually we were very happy with her. She was dignified but lively and amusing. Granny reminisced, however, and sometimes we got bored. We were not supposed to jump about or fidget much and Granny told us we must 'cultivate repose'."

"Florence used to lighten up the conversation and play games with us. She was an absolute joy. Sometimes she dressed us up in Granny's old ball dresses, and on occasion, she made us toys. I remember waking up one afternoon, after a rest, and looking out of the window and down onto the lawn. There was a big hedge and three horses' heads were sticking out of it. These were three hobby horses which Florence had made for us."

"She had made them out of broomsticks. Each horse's head was of material, stuffed, and Florence had pushed a broomstick into each head. There was a little cross-bar at the back. We rode them and enjoyed ourselves."

"Florence was a good illustrator. Once, to amuse us after we had had colds, she made for us some beautifully written scrolls. I was made a "Member of the Order of the Onion" and my scroll had a beautiful picture of an onion at the bottom. My sister, Colin, was made a "Member of the Order of the Pansy.""

The troubles of the 1920s were not very evident in Killiney. But Sheila Stewart recalls that her mother was worried about her Irish husband because he sounded rather English. He had been at school in England and in the Royal Navy. "Going in and out of Dublin, ten miles away, by train, he could have been mistaken for an Englishman, which was dangerous."

"Granny never mentioned the troubles. There was a big palm tree outside my parents' bedroom window, which rustled in the wind at night. My mother used to hope that no one was climbing up to get on to their balcony."

Florence's long stay in Ireland made quite an impact on her. I, her niece, remember that she would come home with quite an Irish accent! She would sing "Phil the Fluter's Ball" to me. She quite liked drinking Guinness, after an Irish doctor had recommended it to her as a tonic after 'flu.

The sea crossing from Holyhead could be very rough and could delay you. As a child, I often heard that Auntie Flo had "missed her connection" home, by boat train, after a stormy passage over the Irish Sea.

As she became older, Florence's lady, Mrs. Edith Martin, was not always an easy person to live with. She had her mild eccentricities, as Sheila Stewart relates: "Granny Martin was afraid of being cold. Someone told her that newspaper was awfully good for keeping you warm."

"She got hold of the Daily Mail and asked Florence to put

red flannel on one side of it and black satin on to the other side. Then it had four tapes. She used to put it on her back, under her coat, and tie the tapes in front."

"One day in London, Granny Martin was walking down Bond Street and her homemade insulator fell off. She wasn't going to admit that it was hers in the street, there and then. But when she arrived home she asked Florence to make another like it. Florence was wonderful and obligingly made another 'back protector'."

Florence had other gifts which she had to exercise from time to time. Her common sense and her powers of persuasion were needed as Mrs. Martin reached her eighties and used to get worried and depressed.

"One day, Florence turned a chair round, stood on the seat, and pretended she was in the pulpit. She preached to Mrs. Martin that it was one's duty to be happy. She and Mrs. Martin were devoted to each other."

"Granny didn't like people to give her advice but she would sometimes take it from Florence and cheer up. Granny's old diaries repeatedly state: 'I don't think my money will last me out.' Towards the end, Florence must have had a rather hard life."

Large black hats were worn by Mrs. Martin. In the car, she tied a veil over her hat and under her chin. When she was a very old lady, she asked Florence to take to pieces all her old ball dresses. They were packed away in a big trunk where they remained until the death of her daughter, Mrs. Stewart.

Sheila Stewart then rescued them and offered them to a local Women's Institute who sewed the dresses together again. They became appropriate costumes for old-fashioned Music Hall concerts.

In later years, after the second world war, Florence would still stay, from time to time, with the Stewart family. "Florence was a terrific help to us all whenever she came to stay with us," says Sheila Stewart. "She could turn her hand to anything. Occasionally, she could cook.

Mainly, she looked after my mother's clothes and made curtains, or she was just a delightful companion for my mother."

"Florence was always happy and helpful. She was sometimes called upon in an emergency when Sylvia's sister broke her arm, for instance. We were very grateful to her. She and my mother loved being together and it meant that I could have a holiday knowing that my mother, then over eighty herself, was looked after."

"At Sunnybank in Overbury, Florence was always fitting in with everything. Sylvia, my cousin, remembers her walking about and talking while she mended a big Shetland shawl which Mrs. Martin liked to wear."

Now Florence takes up the story. "The house where we lived, in Killiney, was called Otago and belonged to an old lady. She was an aunt of Sir Ernest Shackleton, the explorer. We lived with her until she died, then Mrs. Martin bought the house. We came over to England about three times a year."

"We used to stay sometimes with Mrs. Martin's very great friend, Miss Hogg, in the house at Berry Head, Brixham. This had been the home of the Reverend Henry Francis Lyte, the author of the hymn, "Abide with me". He wrote it, sitting on the headland before he left Brixham for good. He went abroad for his health."

"He was Miss Hogg's uncle. She had the original copy of the hymn in a drawer in her bedroom. Miss Hogg was an invalid. She had been in bed for years. When I used to go in and see her, she was as white as her sheets."

"She always said to me, 'Florence, would you like to see the hymn?' So I would go to the drawer and get the hymn out and read it through with her and put it back again. The original is now in All Saints' church in Brixham, where the Reverend Lyte was Vicar."

Let Sheila Stewart have the last word on Florence. "She was a wonderful person to have had all her memorable experiences because she had such a marvelous memory. She had a lovely sense of humour and was a great character."

*Florence at her 90<sup>th</sup> Birthday Party. She is wearing the brooch presented to her by the Queen. Photos: Richard Lyntton (Né: Richard Bramford)*

*TOP: The Queen Mother with her staff in Southern Rhodesia.
Florence stands in the second row, far right.*

*Florence, far left, with colleagues during a Royal tour in Australia.*

*TOP LEFT: Florence sets off on her travels, in her fifties.*

*TOP RIGHT: Florence with Lady Pamela Mountbatten, now Lady Pamela Hicks, during the World tour made by Queen Elizabeth II in 1954.*

*BOTTOM: King George VI, Queen Elizabeth, Princess Elizabeth, and Princess Margaret on their visit to South Africa in 1947.*

*The Royal tour group features Florence Bramford (circled)*
*with King George VI, Queen Elizabeth I, Princess Elizabeth*
*(Queen Elizabeth II), and Princess Margaret on*
H.M.S. Vanguard *en route to South Africa in 1947.*

TOP: *Florence in her thirties in Ireland.*

*George Bramford, Chauffeur to Lady Johnson of The Hill,*
*Upton upon Severn. This is her Daimler in 1913*

*Florence Bramford, aged 20.*

*This Donkey Cart won second prize at celebrations in
Upton upon Severn for the Coronation of Edward VII
in 1903. My Aunt Mabel holds the reins, Florence is
behind her. The others are the children of Mr. Watkins,
the Blacksmith, who made the arch over the cart.*

*TOP: Florence, aged four, at the Cottage, with her parents,*
*her brother, George, and baby sister, Mabel.*

*Upton upon Severn Infant School, 1908*

# 10 ~ Royal Residences

A fter the death of her motherly employer, Mrs. Martin, in 1935, Florence helped to pack up the Martin home in Ireland and went back to her own home in Worcestershire. She was at home for six months, without employment.

One of the Martin family dissuaded her from becoming lady's maid yet again to the two elderly Miss Bromley Martins, the very ladies who had taught Florence in Sunday school, Miss Madge and Miss Susan. "You need some young life", she was told. This good advice was well-timed.

A letter came one day from Lady Agnes Peel of Blounts, near Reading. Lady Agnes had been born Lady Agnes Lygon, and brought up as the sister of Lord Beauchamp at Madresfield Court, in Worcestershire. She had heard that Florence was seeking a post as lady's maid and she proposed that Florence should go as her lady's maid "on approval" for a month, because her present lady's maid was to be married.

Florence stayed with Lady Agnes for six years, shuttling frequently by train, between Blounts and the Peels' large London house in Belgrave Square. The Honourable George Peel, husband of Lady Agnes, was a grandson of the famous Prime Minister of the Victorian era, Sir Robert Peel.

During the years of the Second World War, Lady Delia Peel, sister-in-law of Lady Agnes, came to Blounts to live. Her own home, Barton, in Norfolk, had been commandeered by the government as a prisoner of war hostel. Numerous Italian prisoners were in residence, making baskets out of Norfolk reeds, bundles of which were eventually found, drying under floorboards, when Lady Delia returned at the end of the war.

In March 1939, an invitation came from Buckingham Palace, asking Lady Delia Peel to become Woman of the Bedchamber to Queen Elizabeth, consort of King George VI. Lady Delia accepted, and in her turn, she invited Florence Bramford to accompany her to Buckingham Palace at Christmas in 1939 as her Lady's Maid and Dresser.

Thus began, for Florence, thirty years' service of being attached to the Royal Household, accompanying a great number of Ladies in Waiting over that period. They served Queen Elizabeth the Queen Mother when she was Queen, and they served the present Queen.

Ladies in Waiting are generally in attendance on Her Majesty the Queen for two or three weeks at a time. Her Majesty has a number of Ladies and Women of the Bedchamber to call upon. They accompany her, in the background on all her engagements. They go on royal tours abroad.

The Lady in Waiting must attend to Her Majesty's personal needs at public functions, but the Queen also has her own maid and dresser. The Lady in Waiting is a companion in a position of trust, who will share the Queen's daily experiences with the same stamina, poise and good humour as is constantly displayed by Her Majesty, during her arduous programs.

A Lady in Waiting must not dress to outshine the Queen, but she will certainly take with her to the royal residences her family jewelry and tiara, ready for a banquet in honour of a visiting Head of State. She deals with the Queen's private correspondence and goes shopping with Her Majesty.

Florence gradually came to know the Housekeepers of all the royal residences, and many of the other dressers, valets, footmen, secretaries and chauffeurs attached to the Royal Household.

If her Lady was "in waiting" in January, Florence would accompany her to Sandringham, Norfolk, where the Queen and her family habitually reside in the New Year. Sometimes she would be at Buckingham Palace; or at Clarence House, where the Queen Mother was later to reside after the death of King George VI. For Ascot week in June, the Queen and her household would be at Windsor Castle.

In August or September, Florence would join her Lady in Waiting in Scotland, travelling by over-night train to Balmoral, where the royal family spend their summer holidays. She remembered staying at Balmoral regularly for thirty years, but with different Ladies in Waiting.

In a colour photo of the facade of this royal residence, Florence would point out "her" bedroom window and the portion of the garden where she and other staff would sit on fine days. And she would recall walks on the hills among the heather.

"At Balmoral the red squirrels were tame," said Florence. "They would come on the flat roof and we would feed them on rock cakes specially made for them by the cook!"

Even in her nineties, Florence still received postcards from her Ladies staying in Balmoral "I do wish you were there at the end of the corridor." "Lots of fishing and picnics here every day."

Florence often stayed at Birkhall, the Queen Mother's residence in Scotland. Once, she stayed at Glarnis, home of the Queen Mother's parents, the Earl and Countess of Strathmore. The Earl was ill and the Queen Mother was visiting him. They went there by car from Balmoral, through Kirriemuir.

"Glamis is a lovely house and estate," said Florence. "Another dresser and I were given a room in one of the towers, so we called ourselves 'The Princesses in the Tower'!"

Florence was always entertaining others, sharing her fund of rhymes, sayings and amusing anecdotes with all whom she met, whether Ladies in Waiting, dressers or valets. She was delighted to be doing such a fascinating job in unusual places a job that demanded precision in timing and performance and great dedication.

But it was all such fun! Travelling to different parts of the country; catching sight of the Queen in evening dress and tiara, as she set out for a visit to a Covent Garden opera; chancing to see the Queen Mother arrive home after an exciting day at the races.

Florence had some interesting memories of royal residences during the second World War.

She was in Buckingham Palace when a bomb exploded in Green Park and the whole Palace shook. She remembered the picture hooks clattering down from the picture rails onto the uncarpeted floors of the corridors. Pictures and carpets had already been stored elsewhere, for safety. She recalled that they had meals while sitting at tables in the corridors the most protected parts of the building.

"So many windows of the Palace were boarded up that we could not see well in the darkened rooms. We were oblivious of the weather outside. One day, I emerged from the Palace to find, to my surprise, that it was snowing heavily!"

King George VI and Queen Elizabeth went every night to Windsor Castle to sleep. The two princesses were living there during most of the war years, away from London's bombs.

In the evenings, in Windsor Castle, Florence and her Lady

in Waiting would see Nanny Knight and the young Princess Margaret, then aged about ten, in the darkened corridor. They were waiting to go down in the lift to the cellars, where all the air-raid shelters were located. Princess Margaret always carried a small case containing her treasures.

Florence and the other staff would then go down to their area of the cellars to sleep. In the beginning, they slept on mattresses. Later on, they had bunk beds.

One day, at Windsor Castle, they saw a mock air raid incident, staged by Air Raid Wardens, when the "wounded" were brought in to be bandaged. The two princesses were watching, as a "bad stretcher case" came past. Florence heard the young Princess Margaret ask anxiously, "Is he really badly wounded?"

# 11 ~ The First Royal Tour— South Africa 1947

• • • • • • • • • • • • • • • • • • •

Great Britain was still recovering from the effects of the Second World War. There was still food rationing and shortages of all kinds when battleship *H.M.S. Vanguard* sailed from Portsmouth on February 1ˢᵗ 1947, for South Africa, carrying King George VI, his consort, Queen Elizabeth, the Princesses Elizabeth and Margaret, and numerous members of their Royal Household.

Some Britons criticized the timing of this tour, envious of the Royal Family, who, they thought were off to enjoy a "holiday in the sun", in beautiful scenery with plentiful food.

Little did they realize what a demanding tour this would be. There were two months of constant travel from Cape Town to Southern Rhodesia, in the White Train, with frequent stops and endless receptions.

The Royal Family and their staff all had to work hard, including the two maids to the two Ladies in Waiting, in Carriage 5, Compartment B. One of these Maids or Dressers was Florence Bramford.

First came the long sea journey. It was very strange living on a battleship for seventeen days. There was a crew of 1800 onboard. "We were guarded day and night by a sailor outside our door and escorted everywhere," Florence recalled.

"I was looking after Lady Delia Peel. We had to use an outside gangway to go from our quarters up to the Ladies' quarters. One day, I was going up, carrying a dress on a hanger, and holding on to the rail with the other hand, to keep myself from being blown away. All of a sudden my dress came right up over my head!"

"One of our party was down below and he called out to me, 'My goodness, Miss Bramford, you've got the wind in your sails today!' And I was feeling very embarrassed because of what I was showing!"

Highlight of the voyage was the elaborate "Crossing the Line" ceremony at the Equator. "The night before, the Vanguard was halted and Father Neptune came aboard to announce that ceremonies would have to start tomorrow, in his domain."

"So they prepared a huge tank of water and all the people who hadn't crossed the Line before had to be lathered on their faces, shaved with a great big wooden razor and dipped in the tank."

Fireworks began the lengthy pantomime, according to Florence's official program of the occasion. Crowds of sailors participated, dressed as bears, barbers and pirates. Dolphinius, clerk to His Most Oceanic Majesty, preceded King Neptune and his Queen.

The whole ceremony was proclaimed in verse. Royal Equerries were ducked by the "bears". Their Britannic Majesties were spared, having crossed the Line before.

The Princesses had their noses powdered and were given a cherry to eat they got off lightly!

Florence told me: "A lot of 'our' men staff were hiding, but the bears fished them out and dipped them with their clothes on! The ladies of the Royal Household were not dipped."

"Instead, Father Neptune hung round our necks The Order of the Starfish which I've still got upstairs a wooden starfish on a ribbon." Florence always treasured this Order and kept it on her dressing table.

"Afterwards, there were so many sailors who hadn't been dipped, that they put the hose pipe on them and the decks were awash. That was their Crossing of the Line!" Florence had clear memories of living on the White Train in South Africa and how the red dust got into everything.

At each stop, an army of cleaners descended upon the train with buckets and mops.

The train's fourteen coaches (six had been built in England and brought out in small ships), wound their way through the dusty countryside. They were preceded by the "Pilot Train", on which travelled the police, press correspondents, photographers and the man who supervised flower arrangements in the royal apartments bowls of roses.

Florence recalled: "At one Government House, the rails ran into the kitchen garden, so we stepped off among the cabbages and lettuces! Of course, at each halt, besides cleaning the train, they fixed new generators for lighting and heating water, and replaced the loo buckets. There were two engines in front and one behind, and the South African train drivers wore white overalls."

The centre carriage of this superb train comprised an office for the King, who still had documents and letters to sign. There was a dining room and sitting room for the Royal Family, next to their bedrooms and bathrooms.

"It was really a marvelous train," Florence used to say. "Lovely coaches and very comfortable. All our heavy luggage was kept in the baggage wagon, in the last coach of the train."

"Every time we stopped, we nearly always had to go and get something out of the luggage for our Ladies. Different places wanted different clothes. We couldn't keep them all on the train because there wasn't room."

"I had to share my compartment with Miss Geach, Lady Harlech's Maid. I said to her, 'I'm going to fix up somewhere where we can hang our own clothes'. So I got a piece of string and I put it along the rack. Our suitcases were on the racks and we hung all our dresses up on the string on hangers, under the racks."

"I had a sheet which I hung over the top. At night, I used to tie this sheet back with another piece of string, so that I could get into my bunk. In the daytime, I let it flow down so that the dresses could flow free. We lived on that train for more than six weeks." Florence was always resourceful!

This marathon Royal Tour ended on April 25th 1947. By then, the royal party had endured a journey of 6,000 miles in the White Train, 2,000 miles by car and 800 by air. They had attended innumerable receptions, balls, state banquets and seen ostrich farms, game parks and countless tribal dances. It had been an immense test of endurance for them all, including their staff.

# 12 ~ Royal Tours— Memorable Moments & Hazardous Happenings

Every hour of a Royal Tour is planned meticulously beforehand even the exact departure time of the luggage. Packing and unpacking is an important duty of a Lady's Maid, or of a valet.

Florence Bramford was well known to her various Ladies in Waiting as "a marvelous packer". She would fold dresses carefully round new tissue paper or use pages of magazines to keep outer garments in shape. Transparent polythene bags were a godsend for wrapping smaller items of underwear and locating them easily.

As for jewelry, Florence would have to collect her Lady's tiara and other jewelry from a bank safe, for a period of Waiting on the Queen, and carry it with her in a special case, wherever she went. Once, Florence had to take a diamond tiara to bed with her, for safety, as there was no access to a safe until morning.

In Kingston, Jamaica, a Jamaican bodyguard asked Princess Margaret's Dresser if he could have the Princess's jewelry to lock away. He was under the mistaken impression that it was his responsibility. Florence heard the indignant Dresser reply, "Over my dead body!" A Lady's Maid is also responsible for repairing and cleaning the dresses of her Lady, while on tour. In Jamaica, there was an evening reception at King's House. Lady Pamela Mountbatten wearing a long blue taffeta dress, about six yards round the hem., had been walking over dewy grass and sandy paths. She discovered later, to her dismay, that her dress had a watermark of brown sand round the hem.

Florence remembered Lady Pamela's exclamation on the morrow. 'Oh, Miss Bramford, my dress is ruined!' 'Well', said Florence, 'I'll have a go at it later on'. "So I had it hanging up over my basin and I used to wash it so far every day. Finally, I got round the whole hem and got all the sand out. Lady Pamela was very pleased otherwise the dress would have been a write-off."

Another crisis involved a dress stained with motor oil, in Panama. Owing to the exuberant crowds breaking ranks, one of the Ladies had been forced to move among the motorcycle escort and had a black greasy mark on the hem. Florence remembered that "Tide" had been used once, onboard ship, to eradicate a tar stain. So she used this successfully on the oily mark.

Zips too caused problems. "Lady Delia Peel came back to the White Train with a burst zip. So she had to put on another dress. I got a new zip in Capetown and sewed it in," said Florence calmly. (see Footnote 1)

---

Footnote 1: When "Worth" were asked to renovate the dresses belonging to one of Florence's Ladies, after a long Royal Tour, they sent a message, which was conveyed to Florence: "We have never had clothes returned in such beautiful condition before." Florence's cleaning, pressing and mending was esteemed by everyone concerned.

"We were in Rome once, on a State visit, when a zip stuck in the dress being worn by Lady Abel Smith. The Italian Housekeeper of the hotel came up and said, 'I'll get your dress taken to one of the dress-making houses in the city, for a new zip'. So she had it in a box and it was brought back as good as new next morning."

Laundering dresses en route could create another worry. In Brisbane, Australia, it was too humid to dry anything. So Florence put her Lady's white gloves to dry in the airing cupboard, where there was a glow from an electric light. Otherwise, she made her own laundry line hanging from balconies.

"In Ceylon, we went up into the hills for the weekend, on a special train, laid on by a Ceylon tea plantation owner. He wanted to return hospitality to the Queen, after the wonderful time he had enjoyed at her Coronation in London in 1953. So we had a lovely rest up there, all of us, out of the heat."

"Then a notice came round to our rooms to say, 'Any dresses to be washed or gloves to be cleaned should be put out in the morning and they will be returned in the evening'. I was with Lady Pamela Mountbatten, so I put out six dresses of hers, four of my own and some gloves of hers. They were all washed and brought back that night. Marvelous really!"

"The irons and ironing boards were always there before us. As soon as we arrived at our destination, we could plug in an iron and get our Lady's dress ready for the evening reception.

"Who or why or where or what
Is the Akund of Swat?"

asks Edward Lear. Florence was soon to find out!

The kingdom of Swat, a valley in Pakistan, was secluded, until 1895, when the British broke in. Alexander the Great had been there before them. Snowy peaks contrast with the churning rivers and vivid greenery. The nomads, herding goats, are friendly, but wary. Husbands are still likely to beat wives.

Their leader, The Wali, relinquished his title in about 1969. He had built roads, hospitals and schools by then, so could afford to sit in his palace, puffing at his cigar. The Akund, of Lear's poem, came from a herdsman family and was revered as a saint. His tomb became a place of pilgrimage.

Florence recalled Swat. "In India, we went from 'boiling' Delhi up to the Kingdom of Swat in the mountains—very cold on the snow-line. We had to have log fires in our rooms to keep us warm and we had to wear our coats inside the palace."

"A little man used to come round and see the logs were all right. He would stand and watch me ironing the knickers. "Fascinated he was, because all the women there were in purdah and never came out of their houses at all.

It was all men in the streets."

"I was talking to one of the men and I said, 'Why do they shut themselves up?' He said, 'The women are allowed now to come out. But I can't get my wife out. She won't come at all!' Very funny it was!"

When visiting the Vatican in Rome, the present Queen took with her six staff Maids and valets. Florence was one of these. They all carried the change of clothes needed by the Queen and the Duke of Edinburgh for an audience with the Pope.

The Duke and his equerry wore knee-breeches and a cutaway coat. The Queen and her Lady in Waiting wore black dresses, a tiara for the Queen and black veils. The staff, meanwhile, all had lunch outside, in the lovely Vatican garden.

Black dresses are always taken on Royal Tours in case they are needed for mourning. Once, at Balmoral, Princess Margaret heard that Florence had been pressing the black dress of her Lady.

She was anticipating that King Gustav of Sweden, who was very ill, should die. The premature ironing of the black dress caused the Princess to assume, mistakenly, that King Gustav of Sweden had already died!

When in South Africa, a Lady in Waiting had asked Florence to bring out from her luggage her black dress 'just in case'. Florence had replied, "Oh no, you'll bring on a funeral!" But the Lady in Waiting persisted. The next day they heard that the King of Denmark had indeed died, so they had to wear half-mourning for a week. No one blamed the Lady in Waiting!

Florence made friends wherever she went. In Pretoria, Lady Delia Peel and Florence had to stay for four days in the house of Field Marshal Smuts, because there was no room in Government House. Florence remembered that at the close of the reception, a South African lady rushed forward to get hold of the glass from which the Queen had been drinking. She said she wanted to keep it in her cupboard forever!

Field Marshal Smuts' English steward had an Afrikaans wife. "Very nice people they were, Mr. and Mrs. Marsh, and they took a fancy to me. I saw them again, years later, in Bulawayo, when l was out there with the Queen Mother. I used to write to them every Christmas until they died."

Godfrey Talbot was the BBC correspondent on countless

Royal Tours. Florence would often see him sitting on steps 'talking into his little box.'

In the Nandi Hills, in India, the Ladies' Maids were given the chance of visiting a temple. None of them wanted to go, except Florence, who was game for anything. She went off in a car with "the boys" the valets and footmen.

They all had to take off their shoes to enter the temple. Outside, there was a very old man sitting by the door. Someone found out that it was his 90th birthday. So Florence and her friends all sang "Happy Birthday" and "For he's a jolly good fellow."

But it was not all honey, being on tour. Besides adapting to extremes of climate, there were the unpredictable elements and consequent delays, which tested one's stamina and flexibility.

Florence remembered how they were twice struck by lightning. In South Africa, the White Train had stopped for meals to be taken and generators were being recharged. A loud bang announced the lightning, but fuses were soon repaired by the ever-present South African engineers.

Lightning struck again, in the Pacific, at 5 am, en route for Fiji, and they were deprived of electricity for a while. From the deck of *H.M.Y. Britannia*, they used to watch the sheet lightning as midnight approached.

Floodlighting on a later tour of South Africa proved to be too heavy a 'load' for the town's normal electricity supplies. The power went off. 'Mr. Henry', the Queen's hairdresser, hastily had to finish setting one Lady's hair and put on her tiara by candlelight. Elsewhere, another Lady had to dry her long hair in the warm sun because the power was off.

Mr. Henry Joerin, the Queen's hairdresser, often used to help Florence carry the heavy case of the Mountbatten jewels during the Queen's six-month world tour in 1953–54. He accompanied Florence round Delhi and Rome, during their "time off".

Fog at London airport once postponed take-off of the royal plane at the beginning of a tour abroad. When the royal party, at last, took off, in a cold plane, the delayed breakfast was served at 11.30 am with a warming glass of sherry.

On one occasion, Florence and another Dresser had to travel in a baggage plane with luggage. It was very draughty during the two-hour flight. Seeing some newspapers on the floor, they wrapped these round them before putting on their raincoats. Even then, they were frozen.

Florence said, "I always used to carry a flask of brandy in my handbag after that. Once, flying over Khatmandu, it was so cold absolutely bitter. A colleague said to me, 'What would I do for something to drink, to warm me up!' I replied, 'Well, you needn't worry. I've got something here'."

"So I took out my little bottle of brandy and the Queen's Page, who was there as well, said, 'Oh Flo, how kind of you to bring that!' So my colleague had a swig and he had a swig and I had a swig and we all felt much better. It warmed us up, I can tell you!"

"In Nepal, we had all our meals out of doors on a verandah. Our rooms were over the stables. But there was no proper "loo" just a hole in the floor. I was with Lady … She was staying in the palace nearby. I said to her, 'Please can I use your "loo"?' She replied, 'Of course, you can! Whenever you want to. I know all about those holes!'"

The shortest ever Royal Tour was curtailed in Kenya in January 1952. Florence and the others had just arrived at Mombasa and had unpacked for their Ladies and Equerries. The Queen's Page said he would meet them with a car and take them to a beach.

He was very late in arriving and when he did appear, he told them the sad news that King George VI had just died and that they must re-pack at once. This took them far into the night because they had to leave early the next morning to return to London.

Meanwhile, at Treetops, Princess Elizabeth, with the Duke of Edinburgh, had just received the awesome news that she was now Queen Elizabeth II.

Florence was always happy to return home to her Worcestershire cottage when off duty. There, in peaceful surroundings, she could recover from the demands of her responsible job. She could rest after the long journeys in all kinds of climates. She could be looked after by her younger sister, Winifred, who was a good cook.

In the cottage garden, Florence would sit, on a sunny day, peeling potatoes or sewing, just as she had done as a girl. She could recall all her exciting travel adventures, while, nearby, the hens clucked and the bantam cock crowed.

Her sister's corgis and white cats with green eyes would lie at her feet. One cat was called Timoshenko, after a Russian admiral in Hitler's war. A Polish goose, named Martha, was a good "watchdog" and lived for 22 years. There were goats too.

The two sisters would often cycle ten miles, with friends, via Longdon Marsh, to the southern end of the Malvern hills, for a picnic in bluebell woods, at White Leaved Oak. Regularly, they would cycle to Great Malvern, in all weathers, to shop for groceries, which would travel home in their bicycle baskets.

Florence told me, "Lady ... was scheduled to go to Canada with the Queen but her Dresser was unable to go. Lady .... phoned me one Thursday and said, 'Can you come with me to Canada on Monday? And can you come and do my packing on Sunday?'"

"I agreed to accompany her to Canada and had to go to London on the Saturday which left me with scarcely two days to get ready from scratch. Very short notice, really!"

But Florence was always ready for anything.

# 13 ~ Kings and Queens Are Human!

• • • • • • • • • • • • •

When Florence first went to Buckingham Palace, she got lost. Unknowingly, she was walking along the wrong corridor, on a floor above or below her Lady in Waiting's room.

She opened a door and found to her dismay that she was actually in the sitting room of Queen Elizabeth, consort of King George VI and that the Queen was sitting there with her Dresser. Overcome with awe and discomfiture, Florence began to back out, murmuring profuse apologies.

But Queen Elizabeth, now the Queen Mother, smiled, put Florence at her ease, and asked her Dresser to accompany the lost Lady's Maid to the room of her own Lady in Waiting.

"We were out in New Zealand once," said Florence, "with the Queen Mother, in Hamilton. She was going to a banquet one evening and we were standing in the street, like everybody else, watching her go by."

"She suddenly saw us, because the lights were very bright. She waved at us, from the car's open window. A man standing by us was puzzled. 'You got a good old wave,' he said and seemed quite jealous. He didn't know we belonged to her!"

Florence always associated the Queen Mother with her Castle of Mey. "It's right on the coast. You can see the Orkneys, straight across the Pentland Firth. It's very quiet and restful for her up there."

"We were on *Britannia,* going round Scotland. The Queen Mother sent a message inviting some of us to go there for tea. We went ashore and the Land Rover was waiting for us. We were taken all over the Castle. There's a lovely enclosed garden behind a wall."

Princess Margaret was a favourite with Florence. "She was always very nice. She puts you at your ease at once. I went on a tour with her to the Caribbean, as her second Dresser."

"One day, Princess Margaret said to her regular Dresser, 'I haven't seen Miss Bramford lately, so let her come and dress me tonight.' I went and helped the Princess dress that night. She said, 'I haven't seen you lately.' 'No', I said, 'I've been very busy, Your Royal Highness, busy in the background.' 'Yes,' she said, 'I quite understand'."

"I shall always remember how the Princess had a tray of Caribbean shells on her lap. There were shells of all colours and all shapes, which she had picked up from the beaches. She was arranging them into patterns, and exclaiming how pretty they were."

Florence was asked to look after Princess Anne when the Princess was still a schoolgirl. During five weeks of the Easter holiday from her school at Benenden, Princess Anne was at Windsor Castle. She was an independent young lady, always dressed in jodhpurs, out riding all the time.

Prince Charles, as a little boy, would come into Florence's room, as she was sewing, and would ask what everything in her work-basket was for. Then he would ask, 'And who are you? And what do you do?'

Florence recalled: "When Prince Charles and Princess Anne were children, they would play about on board *Britannia,* the Royal Yacht. The Admiral used to arrange for a game where something was hidden and they had to go and find it. They used to come tearing along all the gangways and in people's cabins and looking under the beds. One day I went into my cabin. There was a sailor on his knees and both the children, looking for something!"

"They used to have these "Sailor Nannies" looking after them in the daytime. Their own Nanny Lightbody couldn't chase about like that. It was quite amusing to see them rushing round, playing football, with two sailors after them."

"Another time, some years later, onboard Britannia, I used to see the Nanny who looked after Princess Margaret's two children, Lord Linley, and Lady Sarah Armstrong-Jones. Little Lady Sarah was being put to bed one night, and her Nanny said, 'I want to go along and see Miss Bramford.' Lady Sarah said, 'Oh, I know! that nice lady with the white hair!'"

Florence's greatest accolade came when she was asked, on one occasion, to look after Her Majesty, Queen Elizabeth II herself, as her personal Maid, for a week, at Sandringham. An emergency had arisen.

Miss Margaret MacDonald is the Queen's personal maid. She has been with the Queen since Her Majesty was a small girl. As she was unable to attend on the Queen on this occasion, Miss MacDonald suggested that they should send for Miss Bramford at once. It appeared that Miss Bramford was the only one to whom Miss MacDonald felt that the Queen could be entrusted in her absence.

But Florence was not on the phone in those days! How was the Royal household to contact her? The Court Post Master said, 'I'll get her through the police.'

Let Florence tell you what happened. "So he rang the police at Upton upon Severn. The police phoned the Rose and Crown, which is the pub next door to our cottage. The landlord came round and told Win, my sister, that she must get me to phone

Windsor Castle at half past-six that evening. But, you see, I wasn't there, at home I was near Reading, staying with a friend."

"So Upton police phoned Reading police and they phoned the village constable. When I found a note from the village Constable, I phoned Windsor Castle. I was to go there almost at once, for Miss MacDonald to show me that weekend how to do things for the Queen."

At Sandringham, Florence was on her own, looking after the Queen for a week. She dressed Her Majesty and attended to her wardrobe, and found it all most interesting.

"The Queen thanked me very much when I came away.

I said I hoped everything had been all right, and she said everything had been perfect. So that was my experience with the Queen!"

Florence never saw Queen Victoria, but she did see the procession of the newly crowned King George V and Queen Mary on the day after their Coronation in June 1911. Everyone remembered that year for its long hot summer when reservoirs shrank to become mere trickles of water. It was the hottest, driest summer since 1714.

Mrs. Edith Martin, Florence's lady in 1911, had booked seats for the Coronation procession, for her friends, at £1 each. These seats were outside a tobacconist's, opposite the Ritz in Piccadilly. Florence's party arrived there by 6.30 am and was given sandwiches (port and beer for the men) until the grand procession came past at 11 am. At last, Florence saw King George V and Queen Mary in an open carriage.

In her old age, Queen Mary would attend the royal family's film shows, at Sandringham, to which members of the Household were also invited. Florence would then whisper to her companions, "This is a Royal Beehive. There are three Queens present today!"

# 14 ~ An Honour Richly Deserved

"The Royal Victorian Order was instituted on the 21st April 1896 as an Order entirely in the gift of Her Majesty Queen Victoria. To enable Her to acknowledge and reward outstanding and personal services rendered unto Her and of which said Order, Her Majesty, Her heirs and successors, were forever to be Sovereigns."

"As a personal gift from The Monarch, admittance to the Order was, and continues to be, held in high regard." In the Court circular of February 3rd 1966, the following appeared:

"Buckingham Palace, February 3rd. Surgeon Vice-Admiral Sir Derek Steele-Perkins had the honour of being received by The Queen on board *H.M. Yacht Britannia* yesterday when Her Majesty invested him with the Insignia of a Knight Commander of the Most Honourable Order of the Bath (Military Division).

*Miss F. Bramford* also had the honour of being received by The Queen when Her Majesty decorated her with the Royal Victorian Medal (Silver)."

To be awarded a personal honour by the Queen in the New Year Honours was exciting enough. To receive such an honour from Her Majesty, onboard the *Britannia*, in Caribbean waters, en route to the West Indies, was a unique occasion indeed. Commander Rodney Bowden pointed this out in his letter of congratulation to Florence. Florence recalled the occasion vividly: "One of the Britannia sailors told me, 'Your medal's coming out with us, onboard. Yes, you're going to get it from the Queen, on *Britannia*.'

"So I had to go to the Queen one evening, after my supper and before her dinner. She was in her sitting room and she presented my medal to me. And the doctor, who always used to travel with us, Admiral Sir Derek Steele-Perkins, he received an order as well."

"I met the Admiral next morning and he said, 'Oh, Miss Bramford, I want to congratulate you. You've made history. The Queen has never given that order on *Britannia* before, so it has gone down in the Log Book.'"

Many were the letters and telegrams of congratulation awaiting Florence when she returned home.

Mr. Henry Joerin, the Queen's hairdresser, wrote from Sandringham: 'I was so pleased to see your name in the Honours List on January 1st.'

'We have been to so many places together, so many odd places, that there is hardly a journey I have made that you were not with us from tropics to the Arctic, by sea, air and train. What a record you have earned! You have deserved your R.V.M. for a long time. My most sincere congratulations.'

One of Florence's Ladies in Waiting wrote, 'Never has an honour been so richly deserved. Indeed, you ought to have the Victoria Cross for putting up with so many tiresome Ladies in Waiting, in so many extraordinary places all over the world! And never do you seem to be unduly worried or put out. We owe you so much. I am so *glad*.'

Florence had already received in 1954 a special brooch from

the Queen, at the end of the royal tour round the world, after the Queen's coronation.

"We were coming up through the Mediterranean, in *H.M.S. Gothic*", recalled Florence. "We joined *Britannia* at Tobruk. It was *Britannia's* maiden voyage to greet us after the world tour. Prince Charles and Princess Anne, as young children, were on board *Britannia,* to greet their parents. On our way up to Malta, the Queen gave us all a brooch to all those who had been on her world tour."

The brooch, cherished and worn by Florence on very special occasions, depicts a white Tudor Rose, surmounted by a crown, representing Queen Elizabeth II. This is flanked by two gilt anchors, symbolic of the naval career of Prince Philip.

Florence continues her recollections: "I was with Lady Pamela Mountbatten (now Lady Pamela Hicks) on the world tour. She was very nice. Her father was then Commander in Chief of the Mediterranean fleet and they were stationed in Malta. He brought the fleet out to meet us. He was swung across by breeches buoy from the flagship to *Britannia.* So we all went up on deck to see the Admiral come across."

"We were still up on deck and all of a sudden I saw Lady Pamela come up the gangway with her father. She was bringing him up to me. They came straight over to me and she said, 'Oh, I want you to meet my father. This is Miss Bramford who has looked after me.' 'Oh,' said Lord Louis, 'I've heard all about you. What a tower of strength you've been to my daughter! She has written and told us all about you.' And he was ever so nice!"

"I had to go ashore in Malta because Lady Pamela was leaving a lot of her dresses there, at Admiralty House. So I had to hang them up in the wardrobes there. Lady Edwina Mountbatten came to chat with me about the Royal Tour which we had just completed. She was very nice."

Florence had travelled on *Britannia* "dozens of times". She used to say, "It's a lovely ship, very comfortable and very well set out. But I've often been sick on it. The first time onboard, they asked us if there were any suggestions to be made for any improvements. I asked for something to hang the hangers on, when we had pressed the dresses."

Her Majesty's Yacht *Britannia* is her home from home on many visits to Commonwealth countries. *Britannia* is captained by an Admiral, appointed for five years at a time.

The royal apartments, decorated in pastel colours, chosen by the Queen, include a drawing-room, where foreign guests are entertained. Prince Albert, husband of Queen Victoria, designed the "gimbel" tables, weighted underneath to withstand rough seas. *Britannia* was fitted with stabilisers after a bad crossing to Sweden.

The Royal Household, comprising equerries, Ladies in Waiting, valets, maids, secretaries, pages, chief stewards etc. are accommodated in 30 or so cabins below the royal apartments.

About 270 crew serve on board, of whom 21 are officers. Their naval uniform has bell-bottom trousers and a special gold flash on the right arm. To eliminate unnecessary noise on board, the crew wear soft-soled pumps, give orders by signaling and are bare-headed. This avoids having to salute. Security onboard is strict, and there is satellite communication.

*H.M.Y. Britannia's* most prestigious moment came, not when the Queen was travelling On her, but fifteen miles off the shores of Aden, on February 17th 1986. The Royal Yacht then rescued 1100 refugees from the Civil War in Aden.

It was an exhilarating occasion. *Britannia* went in 'floodlit and with flags flying'. The rescued, of all nationalities, were thrilled to be allowed refuge in some royal apartments for the brief voyage to Djibouti. This unexpected operation demonstrated that the 'expensive and luxurious' Royal Yacht had fully justified her existence.

In 1958, Florence looked after Lady Hailes. Lord Hailes was about to depart for Trinidad as Governor-General of the newly formed Federation of the British West Indies.

Florence remembered enthusiastically this occasion: "I had a wonderful time with Lady Hailes. I went to pack for her. They were going out to Trinidad for five years. I had all her dresses arriving for her from the shops, because she had an entirely new outfit, right the way through."

"The only thing she left behind in England, in a suitcase, in a store somewhere, was an outfit of black, ready for anyone's funeral. That black outfit consisted of day clothes and one evening dress, shoes and handbag."

"Lady Hailes had thirty boxes of new shoes for Trinidad, and about thirty hats too. And dresses, well! Everything under the sun. All summer dresses, of course. And there were light coats. After all, she was going for five years."

"I had to hang the dresses round the room because I had nowhere else to hang them. I got the pictures all taken down and hung the dresses on the picture rail. Then I covered them up with sheets to keep the smuts off. They thought this a very good idea really!"

"Then we had an entirely new set of suitcases. They were on the landing outside my door and reached right up to the ceiling! There were hat boxes and shoe boxes and goodness knows what. Lovely suitcases, all from Harrods."

"Lord and Lady Hailes had to have their photographs taken, for publicity in Trinidad. So I went with them to the photographer's and took her evening dress and an evening bag and gloves for her to hold. She was in evening dress and Lord Hailes was wearing full dress uniform. This was for the press in Trinidad."

"Lady Hailes badly wanted me to go with them to Trinidad, as her Dresser, but I said I couldn't leave my Ladies. But up to the very last morning, Lord Hailes said, 'Can't you change your mind? You can always follow us on!'"

"They went out on a banana boat. Princess Alice used to go out to Jamaica on a banana boat. It would be a nice sail, really about a fortnight."

Group Captain Peter Townsend, once equerry to King George VI, gave Florence a useful tip for keeping fit. He told her he drank a little TCP antiseptic every day, as a protective disinfectant against germs. Florence thanked him and dutifully drank her daily dose of TCP until her final illness at the age of ninety-four!

# 15 ~ A Mosaic of Memories

● ● ● ● ● ● ● ● ● ● ● ● ● ● ● ● ● ● ● ● ● ● ● ● ● ● ● ●

Florence's family and friends never tired of hearing her re-live her vivid experiences of Royal Tours all over the world. She had been once to South Africa, four times to East Africa, three times to West Africa, twice to Canada and three times to Australia and New Zealand. There were also several State Visits to countries in Europe when she had accompanied Queen Elizabeth II.

Here.are some cameos from Florence's memories.

## KENYA

"When we were with the Queen Mother, the pilot flew us all round the top of Mount Kenya and also round Mount Kilimanjaro to look inside the volcanic crater filled with snow."

## NIGERIA

"In Kano, we were shown round the mud palace of the Emir, who was dressed in green and gold. I was the only one to notice the coloured plates stuck in the mud ceilings and I asked the reason for this. It appears that these plates are put there when the ceiling is made, so they are "baked" into the mud. When the plates fall down, they know it is time to renew the ceiling!"

# GHANA

"That's where I met Rosemary's friend, Pam. She came on to *Britannia*. She was thrilled to bits about that. She was nursing in Ghana and was the only nurse to come on board. I had taken some things out for her from her friend."

"Our detective went to the hospital where she was working and gave her these little parcels I'd taken out. When he came back, he said, 'I've arranged for her to come on board when she comes to the official reception onshore.' So she came on board and spent about half an hour with me and then went ashore to the reception."

"She said the boy who looks after her and wakes her, woke her up at six o'clock in the morning because we were sailing up the coast and we were coming past the hospital. So he woke her up to come and see the *Britannia*. 'They're coming!' he cried. 'Here's the *Britannia!*' This little black boy had woken her up early that morning!"

"President Nkrumah was president then. I was with Lady ... who was Lady in Waiting on that tour. We had to sleep in a little house down in the village. Nkrumah was in Government House, where the Queen was also. But there wasn't room for all of us, so we were in this little cottage."

"I had to go to Government House for all my meals. so I was driven up there, early for breakfast. Lady ... was in bed. When I returned, I used to bring back her breakfast in the car with me, on a tray. I would sit in the car and the Queen's Page would put the tray on my lap."

"The chauffeur had to go very slowly so that the coffee and the milk didn't spill over. I had to balance it, with the car moving in all directions to keep it level. When we got down to the house, the chauffeur would take the tray from me to let me get out. Then I could carry it into the house."

"Lady ... said to me one day, 'Oh, President Nkrumah was asking me if I was comfortable. I told him I was. I said it was very smart having a Rolls Royce to fetch my breakfast! He replied, 'Oh, that's my little Rolls.' Poor old Nkrumah! He's gone! He's spent the money!"

## THE GAMBIA

"We went in barges up the river, where the crocodiles are hunted. It was an all-day trip of seventeen miles."

"The Queen's barge went ahead, but ours was delayed at one point by a fallen tree. We were too high to go under it. We only returned to the Gothic at 8 pm too late to dress our Ladies for dinner."

"So the valets of the party, who were already back on board, joked that they had been combing Lady ...'s hair and they had been running Lady ...'s bath, instead of us!"

## INDIA

"I met Mrs. Ghandi, who was then a Minister in the Indian Government. She accompanied the Queen everywhere in India. Mrs. Ghandi stayed in the same bungalow as Lady Rose Baring and me, in Peshawar. I would see Mrs. Ghandi's manservant bringing out clothes he had pressed for her."

"When we were in Calcutta, Lady Rose Baring's room had a wardrobe which was too small to take her dresses. So I had to be resourceful!"

"I asked a servant to bring me two very large sheets. I placed one of these over the large red screen which shielded the bed, in her spacious bedroom. Then I hung my Lady's dresses on hangers on the screen and protected them from dust with the other sheet."

"Mrs. Ghandi and a woman on her staff came into the room to see that all was well. They congratulated me on my arrangement for hanging the dresses!"

## CEYLON (now SRI LANKA)

"I liked Ceylon very much. We saw a wonderful elephant procession one night, with all sorts of musicians and dancers. They were parading the Buddha's Tooth."

"One ornamented elephant carried the Sacred Tooth and he could only tread on red carpets. So they kept taking up one carpet to put it in front of the other one."

"What slow progress! Men with dustpans cleared up the elephant's droppings."

"I remember that the Queen wore her Coronation gown to open the Ceylon Parliament."

## NEPAL

"It was a wonderful trip to Khatmandu. It looked so lovely in the early morning, from the plane folds and folds of hills. But we never saw Everest. It was always in cloud."

"We stayed in the palace at Khatmandu. The next day we had to go to the King of Nepal's camp, in the foothills of the Himalayas, for a tiger shoot. We didn't see the shoot. There were 120 elephants on this shoot. The Queen was riding on one and the Duke of Edinburgh was on another."

"We heard that the elephants closed in to form a circle to surround the tiger nearer and nearer. But they didn't get a tiger they got a rhinoceros instead! We saw the head of the rhino in the camp that evening."

"The camps consisted of a tent for your bed and another little tent behind for your bath. A tent behind that was your loo. The whole camp had rows of these three little tents. You only had to ring the bell and they came down with a big can of hot water for your bath."

"At night, they lit a very, very big log fire outside and we all sat round. It was a little bit cool because one was glad of a jersey to put on. And then we were entertained by the Gurkhas who did a show for the Queen. They danced and sang and performed all sorts of gymnastics. It was a wonderful show. I thought they were women, you see, because they were dressed up as women but they were all men!"

"In the morning, when we were flying away, our plane took off twenty minutes after the Queen's, so we had quite a good view of the farewell ceremony. All the 120 elephants had come to the airport to see the Queen off. They were all stationed round the airport, facing inwards, to see her go away. It was marvelous. And as we flew away, we could just see them going back into the bush back to their homes."

## AUSTRALIA and NEW ZEALAND

" 'Here come the drones', we heard the Australian crowds say once. They were referring to the Queen's household staff us, as we rode in cars behind the Queen's car! We laughed! We knew we were far from being drones!"

"In New Zealand we saw the little daughters of the

Governor-General, Lord Cobham. They were the two little Miss Lyttelton twins, aged three or four. They came dressed very smartly. We said, 'Oh, you are smart today!' They said, 'We're going to see the Queen Muvver'!"

Florence told me: "I went to see your Auntie Dora in Melbourne, three times. She resembled your mother in every way." This was Florence's sister-in-law, my mother's sister, whom I never met. Dora had emigrated to Australia in 1921 with her husband. She had nine Australian-born children, but she never returned to England.

"Yes," said Florence, "every time I went to Australia, I had tea with Dora. I went in a government car to her flat. The chauffeur was in uniform. Dora's neighbours were impressed and asked the chauffeur to leave the car in *their* drive to impress *their* neighbours! Then they invited the chauffeur and Dora and me into their house and we all had sherry together."

"We sailed to Brisbane and up the Great Barrier Reef for a weekend. This was during the Queen's world tour in 1954. The *Gothic* was lying off the reef. They told us to be sure and wear shoes to wade in the sea because the coral is so dangerous."

"We were put down from a small boat in the sea, and we were up to our waist in water. We waded ashore and looked at shrubs and trees on one of the islands. Then we waded back to the boat over this awful coral!"

## CANADA

"On most Royal Tours, people are pleased to see the Royals, but in Ottawa, some people booed us! From Prince Edward Island, we had sailed in *Britannia* right up the St. Lawrence river to Ottawa. I always remember the maples turning colour.

It was absolutely gorgeous the different shades, from flame to deep gold."

"Once, we were in Edmonton, Alberta, in ice and snow. Our plane, about to take off for Fiji, with the Queen on board, was delayed. Snow had prevented the crew members from arriving from Vancouver. Eventually, we took off, but an hour or so later, we had to turn back to Edmonton, owing to a hurricane near Fiji!"

"A large hotel in Edmonton was given only one hour's notice to prepare rooms for forty people in the Queen's entourage but they managed it! The royal party arrived at the hotel in the early hours of the morning. It was lovely to find the hotel so warm because it was extremely cold outside."

"We had to attend to our Ladies before going to bed, very late. We only had about four hours sleep, as we had to be up for 8 am breakfast, with all our overnight cases packed, ready to take off once more for Fiji."

"Our Canadian taxi driver, who had driven us from the airport to that hotel, said that he and his wife had been playing television Bingo that evening. On the Bingo screen, a notice had appeared: 'All taxi drivers must go to the airport for an emergency involving the Queen'. So he had left his Bingo to rescue us!"

## THE WEST INDIES

"In Jamaica, your Jamaican friends called for me and took me to their home on the sugar estate. There was a banquet for Princess Margaret, at King's House. The bougainvillea is beautiful out there. We saw a large horse-shoe table at the banquet and in the centre, there was nothing but bougainvillea. There were all shades, from deep mauve to purple, and pink, gold, apricot, white like one big cushion, illuminated from below. It was unforgettable."

## TONGA

"We flew from Fiji to Tonga, a small party of us, in a seaplane. We had a wonderful feast in Tonga sucking pig, chicken, duck, melon, bananas, coconuts everything. They had a most marvelous pineapple dessert inside a leaf."

"The table was low and 'T' shaped. At the top sat the Queen and the Duke of Edinburgh, with the Queen of Tonga, Queen Salote. We all sat down below on the ground. At our table, we had Godfrey Talbot of the BBC and all the pressmen. It was rather fun because we got to know them very well."

## AFGHANISTAN

"We were up in the Himalayas, where the camels have their own paths up the mountains. People in villages had made arches for the Queen and they had hung Afghan rugs over them to greet her. The Queen's staff had to go round each arch, as the arches were reserved only for the Queen to pass under."

## PERSIA (now IRAN)

"We saw the Crown jewels of Persia the day after the Queen had seen them. She had told all her staff that they *must* go and see them a sight not to be missed."

"The jewels were kept in a spacious strong room under a bank in Tehran. Many detectives were present. There were trays of rubies, emeralds, diamonds necklaces, tiaras, rings. Where there was a space, this indicated that those jewels were being worn for the Queen's State visit. We saw the Shah's Peacock throne too studded with precious stones a marvelous sight!"

## FRANCE

"We visited Paris in 1938 when President Coty was in office. The French government gave each of us a large book, with coloured photos of the Palace of Versailles, and a huge medallion showing Louis XIV."

## GERMANY

"We had a six-day journey down the Rhine, past all the castles, stopping off at various places. At Munich we all got off the train to have baths!"

"There was a firework display for us in Munich and an enormous crowd in a park. We went out to see the display that night and we had to avoid treading on a dead police horse that had just collapsed at the park entrance. We sailed home from Hamburg in the Royal Yacht, *Britannia.*"

## BELGIUM

"The King of the Belgians shook hands with me on the landing of his country house. We had been first to the palace in Brussels and then we all went on the royal train, lined with blue velvet; to his country residence."

"I was going from Lady Euston's room to my room and a man wearing glasses came along and shook hands with me. I suddenly realised it was King Baudouin, so of course, I gave him a curtsey then. He said he hoped I had been comfortable. I said, 'I enjoyed the train journey and seeing the countryside.'

'Yes,' he said, 'it's very nice here. You'll like it here.' He was a very nice man."

## HOLLAND

"When we were in Holland, Queen Juliana came into the bedroom with Lady Margaret Hay. Lady Margaret said to Queen Juliana, 'This is my Maid.' I did not curtsey to the Dutch Queen, because I remembered that they don't do that in Holland at all. So I just gave Queen Juliana a little bow."

## DENMARK

"I remember seeing the "toy" soldiers in Copenhagen, changing the guard to the music of tinny pipes and drums. They were not a patch on our Life Guards!"

Florence cherished all these memories and she treasured the headed notepaper from all the exotic places where she had stayed during Royal Tours:

Victoria Falls Hotel, Rhodesia

Suva, Fiji

Government Houses in Sydney, Melbourne, Brisbane, Salisbury, Ottawa, Tasmania, Mauritius, Leeward Islands - Bahamas

Moose Lodge, Rotorua, New Zealand

The Residency, Zanzibar

The White Train (Die Wittrein) in South Africa

Kings House, Jamaica ...

wherever she had travelled in the service of Her Majesty, the Queen.

# 16 ~ Still Busy in the Background

Florence was still attending her various Ladies in Waiting in her seventies and well into her eighties. Her invaluable experience as a Dresser, acquired over a lifetime of service, her patience and reliability, her attention to detail were greatly appreciated by her Ladies.

Florence wrote to her family from Windsor Castle in April 1969, at the age of 78:

"We have had a hectic time here, with the Italian State Visit. I saw the table for the State Banquet. It was out of this world. All the gold plate and glass and china and the flowers were beautiful."

"We were full to the brim. The Italians brought quite a lot of people with them. As well as my own Lady to look after, I had the countess of Euston for two nights and Lady Abergavenny for one night."

"Also, I am going with the Countess of Euston for the Prince of Wales's Investiture at Caernarvon. We go up on the Royal Train for two nights. It should be interesting."

The last occasion on which Florence was Dresser to a Lady in Waiting came in January 1974, at Sandringham, when Florence was 83 years old. On notepaper embossed with the Royal Coat of Arms, she wrote from Sandringham:

"I have a bit of cold ... such a lot of it here. One can't help catching it. I shall be glad to get back home old age I suppose.

We are full of Kings and Queens at the moment. What gales we have had here at night nearly blown out of bed!"

Florence's cold became worse and she had 'flu' at Sandringham. A Norfolk taxi brought her all the way home to her Worcestershire cottage to recuperate. She then retired gracefully, but reluctantly from her royal appointment.

But Florence soon recovered and continued to take a lively interest in all the activities of the Royal family whom she had served for thirty-five years. Every day she would read the Court Circular in the Daily Telegraph, to see what the Queen had been doing the day before, and at which royal residence Her Majesty was staying. "You see, I know them all," Florence would say.

Some of her Ladies in Waiting visited Florence in her cottage and stayed to tea. She would receive many a card from a Lady on tour with the Queen 'Wish you were here to pack for us.' She was in touch with several of the Royal Household staff.

Florence celebrated her 90th birthday in the cottage, surrounded by birthday cards. But it was soon time to move out to a more comfortable place to be looked after by someone else. Her sister had died by then.

Adelaide House in West Malvern welcomed Florence, and she had a room with a view looking towards the hills of Wales. Here, she was cared for by a dedicated Warden and domestic staff. Adelaide House is a small Rest Home and is run by the Red Cross.

The lively and pleasant elderly ladies there kept their minds alert with games of bridge, whist and scrabble and were up-to-date with current events and world affairs. They taught Florence, aged 90, to play bridge. Only a few months before she died, she had an unforgettable Grand Slam!

There would be daily walks in the beautiful and well-kept garden; visits from friends, from her nieces or from her Ladies; little outings in friends' cars. Every Christmas, Florence would share with her fellow residents the annual Christmas pudding that she received from the Queen Mother.

Florence herself entertained the "Adelaide" ladies with her ready fund of anecdotes, sayings, rhymes and limericks. She was a born raconteur, having a marvelous memory. She was economical with words and spoke with a fluency vibrant with enthusiasm. Usually, it was an amusing anecdote, for she was always able to see the funny side of a situation.

In April 1983, Princess Margaret was scheduled to open a new wing at Perrins House, Malvern. This is a home run by Friends of the Elderly, of which Princess Margaret is President. Tight security prevailed just then, owing to car bombings. No pressmen, no photographers were to be allowed inside. As soon as the Princess had arrived, the doors were to be locked and the house closely guarded.

But 92-year-old Florence was determined to be present to meet her favourite Princess once more. The Warden of Adelaide House contacted Perrins House to explain the situation. She had to plead with them to allow an outsider to come. Even the taxi driver had to be vouched for and cleared. At last, Florence was sent a "Pass". She rode in the taxi to the ceremony and took her walking aid with her.

The Lord-Lieutenant of the County, Captain Dunn, was told that Florence was present and why. He mentioned to Princess Margaret that Miss Bramford had come specially to see her. "Miss Bramford? Where is she?" said the Princess, surprised and pleased.

The crowd of guests fell silent and stepped back as the Princess walked eagerly to the other end of the long room. She found a dignified old lady, sitting expectantly, dressed in cyclamen pink, and wearing her cherished Queen's brooch.

They chatted about Adelaide House and about Princess Margaret's children. Florence said, "I know a lady who has bought one of Lord Linley's coffee tables." "I must tell him that!" replied the Princess. This was Florence's final royal occasion.

When she was 94, Florence slipped down in the garden, on her daily walk and broke her hip. In hospital at Worcester, they pinned her hip, but she did not walk again, and other complications set in.

Her nieces found Florence sitting up in bed, cheerful, and surrounded by lovely flowers from her Ladies in Waiting. One of them, the Honourable Miss Mary Morrison, devoted to Florence, visited her in hospital, and wrote to us, "I called at Worcester to see her. Despite being in such pain, she was chatting on about the old days and all the old friends at the Palace. She was so marvelous, that day."

Florence's condition worsened, but her mind was still alert. On my last but one visit to the hospital, I remember she was still talking about going on the Blue Train to the French Riviera with Lady Agnes Peel.

The very last time I visited her, I happened to mention Australia. Florence's wonderful memory came back into action and she recalled a vivid image of an Australian white cockatoo which she had seen there, perched on a big sunflower, pecking the seeds. She was still "travelling"!

Florence Bramford died on August 8th 1985, aged 94. A memorial service to celebrate her wonderful life of service was held in St James' Church, West Malvern. Many old friends came, several from her home town, Upton upon Severn.

There were flowers from six of her Ladies in Waiting and a telegram from the Queen and Princess Margaret, who had known Florence since they were children, in wartime.

During the service, Florence's elder niece read an extract from Pilgrim's Progress about the Delectable Mountains. She also read from a Victorian Book of Helpful Thoughts the following passage:

> *"She has achieved success who has lived well, laughed often and loved much; who has gained the respect of intelligent men and the love of little children; who has filled her niche and accomplished her task; who has left the world better than she found it, whether by an improved rose, a perfect poem, or a rescued soul; who has never lacked appreciation of earth's beauty or failed to express it; who has always looked for the best in others and given the best she had; whose life was an inspiration; whose memory a benediction."*

This seemed a fitting commentary on Florence's life.

Her much loved Lady in Waiting declared: "A lovely finale for a very special and marvelous person. She was such a dear friend to me. How much she taught me early on in my job! She was always such a support and help, whether it was at home or abroad, keeping one up to the mark in the nicest possible way."

Florence's colleagues wrote too: "I shall always remember Miss Bramford with great affection, especially her sense of fun. A lovely lady."

Another wrote, "She was such a good sport very popular. We had lots of laughs." Yet another said, "I have so many happy memories of your aunt. She was so good to me on my first tour, being a novice, pointing out what to do and what not to do, and we became such pals on board *Britannia.*"

A friend wrote, "Miss Bramford was always such a sweet, gentle person. I always enjoyed her company." A very old friend said, "She was indeed a Royal subject."

# Epilogue:
## Looking Back Over 90 Years

● ● ● ● ● ● ● ● ● ● ● ● ● ● ● ● ● ● ● ● ● ● ● ● ● ● ● ● ● ●

Florence's vividly recounted assortment of anecdotes bright-
ened many a dull winter's afternoon for her family and
friends. Here is a selection of them:

Lady Agnes Peel took Florence with her to Cannes in the
south of France in the 1930s, to stay in a villa. The French cook
and her husband, who doubled as butler-cum-chauffeur, were
always quarrelling about "Mademoiselle Bicyclette". She was a
French girl who came every day on her bicycle to clean the villa.
Plainly, the cook was jealous of "Mademoiselle Bicyclette".

Florence had to go to the Cannes market to buy three
chamber pots, for use in the bedrooms. She had to carry these
three items home, "naked" and unwrapped, because there was,
of course, no wrapping paper in the marché!

When they visited Grasse, "la ville des parfums", Lady
Agnes Peel asked Florence, "What does this place remind you
of?" Florence looked at the hills and said immediately, "Malvern in Worcestershire—back home!"

With Lady Agnes, Florence also stayed near a lake in
Austria. While she was there, a young man, who came from
Pershore, in Worcestershire, was caught in the reeds, while
swimming in the lake and was drowned.

His parents came over for the funeral. The young man's
grave looked so bare one day, that Florence picked a bunch of

wild flowers, filled an empty jam jar with water, and put these flowers on his grave.

In the 1920s, Florence went with her Mrs. Edith Martin to stay with a lady in Chichester. This lady owned a brewery, so there was homemade beer each day for lunch, for the maids and butler. Florence also enjoyed the quince and apple jam there.

In Brixham, Devon, again with Mrs. Martin, Florence gathered and ate ripe walnuts. She put the shells in a waste paper basket in her bedroom. During the night, she was woken by a sound like the rolling of marbles. It was a mouse rolling the walnut shells across the polished floor!

## LOST AND FOUND

1. Mrs. Johnson, wife of the railway Station Master at Upton upon Severn, had been picking and packing plums, to send by night train to Manchester. Her wedding ring was lost. Possibly it had fallen into a hamper of plums. She informed the Station Master at Manchester. There, they eventually burned the empty hampers and her wedding ring was found, unscathed, among the ashes!

2. One of Florence's Ladies lost her wedding ring, while heaving sheaves of corn. But she never found her ring.

3. An Upton upon Severn farmer found a missing gold cuff-link in debris dumped on his land from a fire at a nearby thatched cottage. A lady lost her ring. Soon afterwards, she gave Florence an old handbag to throw away. Florence wisely searched every part of the handbag first and found the ring! Florence often took her sewing on to the pebbly beach at

Killiney, Co. Dublin. One day, she lost her thimble there. Three days later, she went again to the beach, and as she sat down, she noticed her lost thimble!

4. In Newbridge Green, Upton upon Severn, there was a series of mysterious incidents, when people's washing lines, full of clothes drying, had collapsed and the washing lay soiled on the ground. Watch was kept on Monday washing days. It was discovered that a dog, tugging at the washing on the line, was the culprit!

## TALES ABOUT TRAINS

1. On the night train going to Edinburgh, en route for Balmoral, Florence was woken by the screams of a lady in the bunk above her. On finding that the lady was suffering from cramp, Florence massaged the lady's legs. Years later, in the night train to Edinburgh, a lady in an adjoining bunk said to Florence, "I've met you before." It was the same lady "with the cramp"!

2. Once, on the sleeper to Edinburgh, Florence found she had been booked to share with three men. She objected to the steward, but there was no other compartment available. However, the steward said he would look after her. He made the three men creep into their bunks "like mice", after she had gone to bed. In the morning, he had told them to get up early, so they had disappeared before she got up. The Royal Steward who books train seats and sleepers for the Royal Household was later surprised that the mistake should have occurred at all!

3. Florence knew a child who kept asking his father, "Papa, why is every station called "Kent Lemon?" At last, the father looked out of the train window. It dawned on him that his son was referring to the signs for "Gentlemen"!

4. On a Paris station, Florence got out of the train onto the platform for a little walk. She knew there would be some delay before departing for Cannes. Suddenly she noticed that her train was slowly and noiselessly drawing out of the station already! She hastily climbed in again, only just in time. The train was changing from one Paris station to another.

5. On a French station, Florence noticed two French train guards arguing and putting up their fists. Their "battle" continued for some time. Suddenly, they stopped and kissed one another!

6. One day, in France, a woman asked Florence to carry a parcel through Customs, but Florence refused, politely. Later on, Florence saw this same woman being questioned by the police.

7. On Sandringham station, Queen Elizabeth II was holding little Prince Edward in her arms and she had young Prince Andrew by her side. The Queen was saying to Prince Andrew, "Come and see this lovely steam engine. We shall soon have no more of these." But Prince Andrew was more interested in looking at Florence and others of the Royal Household, who were already on the train!

# FLORENCE'S SAYINGS

"Where's my 'Dr. Who' scarf?" (the very long scarf).

"It's a Thursday day today". This meant "a very cold day when you needed to wear Monday, Tuesday, Wednesday and Thursday layers of clothes."

"It's a 'Boat Race' day" meant "It's a very busy day people going 'in and out' of the house all the time."

When, as children, we would ask her to tell us a story, she would say, "Wait till I put my thinking cap on." We pestered her, in vain, to tell us what colour her cap was and where it came from!

Forgetful parson in the pulpit: I publish the banns of marriage between ... (looking in vain for his notes) Voice from the congregation: ... "between the cushion and the kneeler."

# Rhymes Recited by a Nonagenarian Aunt

There was a Presbyterian cat
A-searching for its prey.
It caught a moose within the hoose
Upon the Sahbbath Day.

The people they were horrifeed
And they were grieved sair
And straightway took that wicked cat
Before the Ministair.

The Ministair he shook his head
And unto her did say
"Oh bad perverted pussy cat
To break the Sahbbath Day!"

"The Sahbbath Day was made for man
An Institush-y-on.
So straightway take that wicked cat
To execush-y-on!"

* * *

My father's friend once came to tea.
He looked and laughed and spoke to me.
Within another week they said
That friendly, pink-faced man was dead.

"So sad," they said, "The best of men!"
I said too, "So sad," but then,
In my heart I thought with pride,
I know a person who has died!

\* \* \*

Tom and Bill they went to law.
Such a sight you never saw.
Tom was deaf and so was Bill,
But the judge was deafer still.

Tom, relating all he'd spent,
Said, "He owes me five months' rent."
Bill replied with smiling scorn
"It is at night I grinds my corn."

Then the judge, serene and bland,
Raised a deprecating hand.
"Why dispute with one another?
After all she is your mother!"

## A Doll From China
(in Blackie's Annual 1911)

Me came floatee
In a boatee,
Muchee wavee plentee.
Voyagee over
Got to Dover,
In a trainee wentee.

Train me whirlee
Right to girlee
English girlee Missee.
Girlee shoutee
Jump aboutee
Give me muchee kissee.

Dolls she's gottee
Waxee, pottee,
Bigee dolls and smallee;
Allee samee
Me she namee
Nicest of them allee.

## London Rhymes

Debenham and Freebody
Met a man named Cedars Peabody.
Said Freebody to Debenham
"That's one of the cedars of Lebanon!"

Swears and Wells
Took a house on the fells.
Wells said to Swears
"There's a ghost upstairs!"

Dickens and Jones
Spoke in grave undertones.
Jones said to Dickens
"Let's go and feed the chickens!"

Bryant and May
Quarrelled one day.
May was defiant
And so was Bryant.

## Naughty Verses and Limericks

I went out with a duchess to tea
I knew just how it would be.
Her rumblings abdominal
Were simply phenomenal
And everyone thought it was me!

\* \* \*

I passed by your window and saw you undress.
I saw you take off both your corsets and vest.
But as I drew nearer the fates were unkind—
You popped on your nightie and pulled down the blind.

\* \* \*

A lady once went to the closet.
She paid the usual deposit.
But when she got there
She only passed air,
So it wasn't a penny worth, was it?

\* \* \*

Here I lie with my three daughters
Who died from drinking Cheltenham waters.
If we'd only kept to Epsom salts
We wouldn't be lying in these 'ere vaults.

\* \* \*

There was a young lady called Maud
Whose appetite was ever a fraud.
To eat at the table
She was quite unable
But out in the kitchen—O Lord!

\* \* \*

There was a young man from Darjeeling
Who travelled on his way to Ealing.
He saw on the door
'don't spit on the floor'
So he promptly spat on the ceiling.

\* \* \*

There was a young man from Nepal
Who went to a fancy dress ball.
He went just for fun
Dressed up as a bun,
But was ate by a dog in the hall.

\* \* \*

There was a young lady from Twickenham
Whose boots were too tight to walk quick in 'em.
She walked for a mile
And sat on a style.
She took off her boots
And was sick in 'em.

\* \* \*

There was an old man who said, 'Well,
Will nobody answer this bell?
I've rung day and night
Till my hair has grown white.
Will nobody answer this bell?'

\* \* \*

There was an archdeacon who said,
'May I take off my gaiters in bed?'
But the Bishop said, 'No!
Wherever you go
You must wear them until you are dead'.

\* \* \*

There was a young lady of Cheadle
Who one day in church sat on a needle.
Though deeply embedded
It was luckily threaded
And quickly pulled out by the beadle.

\* \* \*

There was a young curate of Kidderminster
Who sadly, but surely, chid a spinster.
Because on the ice
Her remarks were not nice
When he accidentally slid ag'inst her.

\* \* \*

There was a young lady of Riga
Who went for a ride on a tiger.
They came back from their ride
With the lady inside
And a smile on the face of the tiger.

\* \* \*

There was an old man of Khartoum
Who kept two black sheep in his room
'They remind me', he said,
'Of friends who are dead',
But he never would tell us of whom.

# FINALE

Florence, whose mother was born in Devon, recited this to her nieces on her last birthday, when she was 94 years old:

I be close on ninety-seven
Born and bred in good old Devon.
There's not a place in all the world
That can compare with Devon.

The Cornish seas be far and wide
But the Devon seas be wider.
And if you'll live as old as I
Take Devon cream and cider.

Thank you for reading
*From Cottage to Palace ~ Book 1*
• • • • • • • • • • • • • • • • • • • • • • • • • • •

For more information about the **Worcestershire & Malvern History Series** by Margaret Bramford, or to sign up for our FREE richardlynttonbooks Reader Regiment newsletter, visit the richardlynttonbooks website:

**https://richardlynttonbooks.com/contact/**

*If you enjoyed the book, we would very much appreciate it if you could leave a review on the platform you used. Thank you so much!*

Made in the USA
Las Vegas, NV
13 November 2022